Girls' Basketball

Building a Winning Program

796.323
KAL

Clay Kallam

Wish Publishing
Terre Haute, Indiana
www.wishpublishing.com

LCCN: 2001099364

Proofread by Heather Lowhorn
Cover designed by Phil Velikan
Cover photography by Painet Inc., www.painetworks.com
Printed in the United States of America
10 9 8 7 6 5 4 3 2

Published in the United States by
Wish Publishing
P.O. Box 10337
Terre Haute, IN 47801, USA
www.wishpublishing.com

Distributed in the United States by
Cardinal Publishers Group
7301 Georgetown Road, Suite 118
Indianapolis, Indiana 46268
www.cardinalpub.com

To Betty Mae and T.C.

Acknowledgments

No book is a one-person production, and this is no exception. I can't possibly thank all those who helped me along the way, but there a few people without whom ...

First, Casey Rush and Scott Brown are the high school coaches I worked with through the '90s, and without their knowledge and support, I would never have been in position to observe what I observed and learn what I learned. Casey and Scott had faith in me, and I can't thank them enough for the opportunity to be involved in their programs and for all they taught me.

Second, my wife Maggi has supported me in all my various endeavors, and she has patiently waited for our ship to come in. ('It's on the horizon ... see that tiny little speck? I promise it'll be docking any day now, and it'll be a lot bigger. OK, so it has oars.')

Finally, thanks to all the players at Monte Vista, Campolindo and Acalanes High Schools who put up with me for all these years. In the end, the game's about the players — the rest of us are just along for the ride.

Table of Contents

Chapter 1
What Color is the End of the Rainbow?

So you've decided you want to coach a varsity girls' high school basketball team. You've had some experience either in CYO or as a freshman or JV coach, and now you're ready for the big step to the head job — and it is a big step. Until you are a head coach, you have no idea what the job is really about and what challenges lie ahead.

It's also important to know why you're about to commit your time, energy and heart to a high school basketball program. Is your daughter on a team that needs a coach? Is it part of a grand plan to become the next Pat Summitt? Or is it a desire to give something back to the game and/or the community?

Regardless of the answer, you have to love basketball — and you have to get a lot of pleasure out of success. For too many coaches, the pain of one loss can offset the joy of 15 wins, and the reality in high school sports is that no one can guarantee a flow of talent that can always go 26-3 and play in the state title game.

Coaching basketball has to be fun, just as it has to be fun for your players. If it isn't, then it's simply not worth it.

But if you are fired up and ready to plunge into the joys and frustrations of building (or maintaining) a high school program, then read on — the road to success starts right here.

The first move isn't to go out and find players or set up feeder programs or go to a Pat Summitt clinic. No, the first thing you have to do is decide how good you can be and how good you want to be.

And like so many decisions you have to make, you can't make it alone. If you want to be a national champion and the administration doesn't, you're doomed to frustration. If you want to be a regional power and the parents don't want to make that kind of commitment, you'll probably wind up butting heads with them and eventually the administration over your demands on the players. And, most likely, you'll either quit or be fired.

So you have to decide what you're aiming for and make sure the players, parents and school administrators are with you. And then you have to be positive you and your family are willing to make the sacrifices necessary to get that far — and trust me, there will be many sacrifices along the way. So consider this rough categorization of high school programs and the commitment involved, and then consider carefully where, and if, you're ready to jump in for a multi-year swim in the sometimes shark-infested pool of girls' basketball.

The Strugglers: This school always loses, and there's a simple reason: No one cares. If there isn't commitment at several levels, then the players pick up a ball for the first time when practice begins, and the coach isn't even sure who's trying out. The best athletes choose other sports, and the parents don't get involved. High schools can get caught in this rut for years, even decades, and it takes commitment and a little luck to get out of it.

If you just want to coach a team and don't care about winning that much, and you don't get upset at players who don't care and sometimes don't try, you might be happy here. You can fit this kind of commitment into basketball season only, and it won't spill over into any other time of year. You can take Thanksgiving and Christmas vacations, while still staying involved in the sport.

Be warned, though: Losing is a lot more corrosive than you think, and it takes a special kind of person to stick this out for any length of time. Almost anyone with any competitive desire at least wants to move up to ...

The Mediocre: Every once in a while, Mediocre High will pull off a big upset — but then will invariably follow that up with a depressing loss. Fads come and go (flex one year, a full court press the next), and often coaches do too. The will to win might be there, but the support system isn't, and the support system (feeder programs, summer teams, camps, etc.) is the difference between mediocrity and success.

The commitment at this level is, despite the marginal improvement in record over the Strugglers, quite a bit greater. Some kind of a summer program is a necessity to have a chance for a big upset, and a few open gyms in the spring and fall are a very good idea. You may want to have a three-week fundamentals' camp during the summer yourself (which can generate some outside income), or you can encourage your players to enroll at others put on by the top schools in your area.

The step from Struggler to Mediocre is a pretty big one, and to be a consistent .500 team will entail a lot of time in the offseason, and six days a week (with limited time off at Thanksgiving and Christmas) during the real season. If you're going to go this far, you might as well try to join ...

The Contenders: Here's a team you might want to go see play. Enough pieces are in place for this school to be in the hunt for a league title almost every season. You can bet there's a summer program that keeps the girls playing the game when school is out, and you know there's a coach who wants to win. The parents are more involved at this level, if only because the demands are greater. The girls are expected to forego Christmas vacations to stay in town to practice, and their parents are expected to drive them to summer tournaments and games. But there's usually a missing element, sometimes as fundamental as talent, but more often it's something more subtle. The coaches may work hard, but not smart. The school may not have an atmosphere of success, or the kids themselves might be a bad mix. Parents, too, can kill a program, either by not getting involved enough or trying to do too much.

Still, Contenders are serious. The coach of a Contender is part of the girls' basketball community and has thought seriously about starting an AAU team in the summer (if it's allowed). There are at least two summer league teams to organize, and the junior varsity coach needs to be strong as well. In fact, a Contender is never a one-person operation. A solid varsity assistant is almost a necessity (the paperwork and media demands start to mount up) and a parent who focuses on fund-raising is someone you can't do without.

The summer season now includes as many games as the regular season, and open gyms and leagues occupy the summer and fall. To keep the talent flowing, attention must be paid to the feeder programs (both scholastic and otherwise), which requires even more time.

The coach of a Contender essentially has added a full-time job to the schedule, and without solid assistants, maybe even more than that. Of course, a Contender gets recognition in the community, and people will treat you and your program with respect. They will also begin to have expectations, but the taste of victory will be very sweet. The team itself becomes a family because the commitment pushes everyone together, and the process is deeper and richer — but equally more exhausting.

Despite this huge commitment, there's still a long way to go. It's a bigger step from Mediocre to Contender than it is from Contender to ...

Regional Power: Though playoff structures vary from state to state, there is almost always a regional/district/ section postseason tournament, and the Regional Powers expect to win those tournaments. In fact, their goal every year is to win the state championship, and though obviously they will fall short more often than not, they still bring the noise every season. These are the teams that put several hundred people in the stands on a regular basis. These are the teams that casual sports fans at the local latté shop know something about. And these are the teams that are very, very serious. From the administration on down, a Regional Power requires commitment. Parents must not only ferry their kids from spot to spot, they must sacrifice money and time to the greater good of the program. The players have to focus on basketball and play other sports only as a hobby. Their lives become wrapped up in the game, for good or ill, and the starters all think seriously about playing in college at some level. The coaches (and by now there are at least two at the varsity level, usually three) are dedicated, even fanatical. As opposed to the Strugglers, the Regional Powers are packed with people who care, and care deeply, about the won-loss record of the school team.

The coach of a Regional Power is, in essence, running a small business. The organization is the same as for a Contender, but the talent level is higher and the pressure is greater. No more time is required (that's hardly possible), but the stress level is greater. Why? There are only two goals for these teams: a state championship, and a leap to ...

The Elite: The difference between an Elite team and a Regional Power can be summed up in one word: talent. An Elite team — that is, a team regularly considered for national rankings — will, most of the time, run at least two future Division I players out on the floor. Public schools

11

must rely on the luck of the draw for that kind of talent to show up, and even private schools can find it hard to keep the top-level players flowing year in and year out. But some do, and after a while, success becomes a self-fulfilling prophecy. The great players gravitate to the Elite schools because a) they want to win, and b) they want to be seen by lots of college coaches. And when the players arrive, they'll find a high school program that often runs at a higher RPM than many NCAA Division II and Division III schools. And, yes, that takes money, which Elite teams must raise in buckets. To be considered for national rankings, it is almost imperative to play in a major tournament (most notably, the Nike Tournament of Champions) and/or go out of state to take on another Elite team.

Elite teams, too, are measured by a different standard. League championships are supposed to be automatic. Regional titles are layups. State titles are expected at least every other year. In fact, the only thing that matters are the national rankings, which means one loss can be devastating.

Because of these expectations, the Elite programs might be the least fun of all, with Regional Powers not far behind. The work load is incredible, the demands grueling, and most of the games are 30-point blowouts. Fans won't see too many exciting finishes unless they travel with the team, and the players and coaches are so inured to success that the joy of 25 wins can't make up for the pain of just one loss.

The head coach is now CEO of a basketball machine. She knows all the local college coaches by name, and her team is in demand by tournaments and one-day shootouts. Games are routinely played at college arenas, and everything is in place for continued glory. Perhaps the hardest thing for a coach at this level is to maintain the level of intensity required, because after a while the rankings and titles tend to become as exciting as new pair of Air Jordans.

There are some significant financial opportunities at this level, mostly in summer camps, and there is also a good chance to move into the college ranks. But to go from Struggler to Elite is a good 10-year process — and requires some serious luck in the talent department. But with the right foundation, it can be done, though it is bound to become an all-consuming avocation.

But maybe the most fun of all is had by the Contenders — or at least those Contenders who are on the brink of breaking through to Regional Power status. For them, wins are joyous, and an upset is cause for wild celebration. There's nothing sweeter than that first state title, unless it's that first win over the nearest Regional Power after years of getting beaten by 25.

And the rewards are much more than just seeing the banner hang in the school gym. A Contender or Regional Power will send girls on to college who might not otherwise have gone, and open doors for others that, without basketball, may have been closed. The players learn what it means to work hard and be rewarded for working hard, and the coaches develop relationships with athletes, parents, community members and the world of basketball that can't be valued in dollars and cents.

It's a hard road, no doubt, and many drop by the wayside. The journey can be exhilirating as well as exhausting — and it makes things a whole lot easier if you have an idea of your destination when you start out. So consider carefully what you want from coaching, and prepare yourself for the commitment, the pleasure and the pain. And above all, remember this hoary piece of coachly wisdom: If you can't enjoy winning, you don't belong in the game.

Chapter 2
First Things First: Where are the Players Coming From?

To win, you need talent. To attract talent, you need to win.

This chicken-and-egg conundrum is one that any new coach must solve in order to build a successful program, but nurturing a steady flow of talent is crucial for even the most established veteran. So, barring an NBA/WNBA breeding program and a very long-term contract, every high school coach must take care of business in two distinct areas: her feeder programs and her relationship with the top athletes in her high school.

Feeder programs come first, and they are the key to any kind of long-term success. It may take a while for them to pay off, but when they do, the wins will inevitably follow.

My first personal debt to feeder programs came when I coached softball at Monte Vista High School in Danville, Cal., but the same principles apply to basketball. This was in the late '70s, when girls' athletics had barely begun, either at the community or interscholastic level. The Monte Vista Mustangs were, when I took over the program, a pretty dismal bunch. There were a few good players, but too many of the girls on the varsity had picked up a bat and ball for the first time when they tried out for the high school team.

I took over at midseason one year, and the team had endured losses in the 43-1 range to the local powers. It was not a pretty sight. It didn't get much prettier during the last weeks of the season, but there were signs of improvement. But it wasn't my coaching genius that made the difference the next few seasons at Monte Vista — rather, it was a local girls' softball league that had begun about five years before. Girls could start playing at age eight, and I was the first coach to benefit from a flood of girls who had actually played softball for several years, and thus didn't need instructions the basics of the game.

My team the following season was filled with freshmen, and the year after that we won the league title. Was it because of my coaching acumen? Well, I'd love to take all the credit, but the truth is that whoever was coaching at Monte Vista would have finally had experienced players to build around — and thus wins were a lot easier to come by.

Youth basketball for girls is well established in many areas, and programs such as CYO start them young. Basketball is a difficult game, demanding a wide variety of physical skills and offering the opportunity for a seemingly endless array of mental errors. The more of those mental errors a girl commits in fifth grade, the less likely she is to repeat them as a junior in high school. Game experience cannot be overemphasized in the development of a basketball player — there is simply no substitute for it. (That said, just because girls have played a lot of games doesn't mean they necessarily have been coached in fundamentals or understand what's going on. Well-meaning parents do the best they can, but it's quite possible for a girl to play five years in a good youth league, and never have learned how to use an arm bar on defense or how to make a left-handed layup. The feeder programs can do a lot, but the coach who expects them to instill a firm grasp of fundamentals is bound to be disappointed.)

The other major feeder program are the local middle schools. Linda Holt, who built Butler High of Huntsville, Ala., into a national champion, started coaching her core group as seventh graders. The group stuck together for six more years, and that extended span of time in the same system — along with a boatload of Division I talent — paid off big time.

As the new high school coach, once you find your mailbox, you should call the middle schools and the local youth league. Get to know the junior high coaches, and find out who the movers and shakers are in the youth leagues. If you can get them excited about your program, then they will get their girls excited about it. And if the girls get excited about playing basketball, they'll work harder to get better. (Not incidentally, they are also less likely to focus on other sports, but we'll get into that later.)

If there are no local youth leagues, you have a problem. You need to try to form one without winding up doing all the work yourself. Your best bet is to find a good young female basketball player and encourage her and her parents to get some kind of league started. It takes years to build a feeder program, but even if you're not around to reap all the benefits, you will have done a lot for area girls — and you will have made some future coach very happy.

Hopefully, a program does exist, and the more you and your players can get involved, the better. Young girls will become very attached to high school girls who ref their games or help out at their practices, and they will come to your games, bringing their parents and buying lots of snacks and soft drinks. If you run a coaching clinic for the local rec league, no matter how few parent coaches show up, you've made some fans, while at the same time you've started to plant your basketball philosophy in the community's athletic garden.

Most junior highs have a basketball program, and it's important to remember that the coaches there are professionals too. They resent someone coming in and telling them how to run their program and what to do. Though in an ideal world, the middle schools would do exactly what you do, the odds of that happening before you win a state title are very small — so be happy if you have an enthusiastic coach who gets a lot of girls out for the team and wins a fair amount of games. Always invite the middle school coaches and their teams to your home games, and if possible, get them in free. The school will make more money on concessions than it will lose on admissions, because a lot of times those kids wouldn't have come if they would have had to pay, but once there, they will head straight to the hot dog stand.

The healthier your feeder systems, the better your talent will be, and the more wins you'll get. As you win more, interest will grow in the feeder systems as parents and girls get enthused about the high school team. With more interest comes more energy, and eventually the feeder programs won't take much of your time at all. But never divorce yourself entirely from the youth leagues and middle schools, because they are the foundation upon which any successful program is built. Without them, the talent will dry into a trickle, and winning will become much harder than it has to be.

There is one more way in which a coach can help herself find talent: Make sure every good athlete on campus plays your sport.

The reality of high school athletics is that there are a lot of sports, and not nearly enough athletes. Those who excel at a particular sport, whether it be football or baseball or basketball or tennis, will play that sport regardless of the quality of the program. That's their game, and they will be the backbone of any successful team, or unsuccessful one.

But the vast majority of good high school athletes aren't scholarship material, and they choose the sport that looks like it will be the most fun or will give them the most back. Usually, the athletes are pretty evenly spread out among the sports, but if you want to make your program shine, you need to do all that you can to attract the best athletes to your team.

That doesn't mean, of course, talking them out of playing other sports, and/or demanding that they only play basketball. Girls need to choose to play basketball because they want to — and often winning is enough motivation. But it should also be clear that you run a quality program, that the players have fun, and that you are part of the school community, and if that message is delivered, athletes will follow.

When all that happens, and you win 20 games a season on a regular basis, your sport will become, in a way, cool, and athletes will be motivated to play basketball when they come to high school rather than soccer or softball. (In fact, they may play all three, but what's important is what sport they play in the summer, not during the school year. If the good athletes do play basketball on your summer league team, and then go out for volleyball in the fall, your program will still be in fine shape. But if none of your players pick up a basketball until the first day of practice, it's going to be a long year — and a short career.)

A perceptive reader may have noticed that after two full chapters on coaching, not an X or an O has been mentioned. In fact, we have a couple more to go before we get to any of that, because real world coaching has a lot more to do with people skills and management skills than technical skills. Supporting existing feeder programs (or building new ones) is all about getting people excited, and getting the best girls to play basketball is all about getting them enthused. Without those two in place, even the most brilliant tactician will find it hard to win games.

You have to have talent to succeed on a regular basis, and it's no accident that one school will have a lot more of it than another. You can have a major influence on your talent flow, and if you like winning (and who doesn't?), then nurturing your feeder programs should be your top priority when you take the job.

Chapter 3
Putting Together a Staff

You're watching a college game on TV — or even a state high school championship and there's one thing that jump right out at you: There is a horde of assistant coaches wandering around. And let me tell you right now, they're not there for show.

The time when one coach could do it all are long gone, if indeed it ever existed. If you're going to have a consistently successful high school program, you need help, and lots of it.

I've talked about nurturing feeder systems, but once the kids get to high school, you need to teach them and inspire them and help them have fun at all levels of play. And that means, simply, you need at least three good coaches to help out at the high school level.

Finding three good coaches who you can work with, and who have similar coaching styles and values, is no easy task. Ideally, you're an on-campus coach, but that doesn't happen as often as it used to for a variety of reasons that we won't go into here. If you're not, and you can find a teacher who wants to coach at the freshmen or junior varsity level, you've hit the jackpot. Connecting with the school is incredibly important, and a teacher who's on campus every day will have a feel for everything from the attitude of the administration to the level of partying going on every weekend.

So start your search there, but look everywhere — even advertise in the local paper (sometimes they'll let you run an announcement in the sports section for free). One word of caution: Try to avoid hiring a parent of a player. We've had great luck with just such a coach in our program in California, but too often the parent is more interested in his or her child (naturally) than the overall program. If the parent wants to coach a different level than his child plays, that's OK, but that also means that many times the coach won't get to see his daughter's games.

Another complicating factor is money. As a head coach, you're presumably infatuated enough with the game and the challenge that the fact you're making 25 cents an hour, in a good year, doesn't bother you. But finding three other people with the same kind of dedication is hard. If possible, you can raise enough money so you can give the extra to your staff, but usually you'll have to accept a limited commitment simply because the dollars don't make enough sense.

In the girls' game, your most important staff member is your junior varsity coach. Because girls mature faster than boys, they are closer to their ultimate physical potential when they enter high school, and a freshman is just about as big as she's going to get. That means she's unlikely to make a quantum leap in raw talent either, which leads to two concepts that someone more familiar with boys' sports will have trouble grasping immediately:

1) A freshman girl can easily start, and even star, at the varsity level. Few boys can handle the jump from junior high because of the extreme physical difference between an 18-year-old and a 14-year-old. For girls, the gap is not that great, and the best freshmen will at worst wind up on the junior varsity.
2) The corollary to that fact of nature is that the girls' freshman team is not going to be the source for

topflight varsity players. Basically, in fact, the girls' frosh are just there to balance out the athletic opportunities for the genders at the high school, and you will seldom get a starter, or even a rotation player, who spent her first year playing freshman basketball.

In terms of the girls' staff, then, your freshman coach is not really going to be feeding you a lot of talent. That means that her job with her team is to have fun with the kids, win some games, and send them back into the school and community with positive feelings about the basketball program as a whole. It is not even necessary that your frosh run the same system as your varsity, though it's still recommended — it makes the freshmen feel like part of the program and it will also smooth the transition of the occasional late bloomer.

But that doesn't mean the frosh coach is a throwaway position. It's a perfect place for a young former player to get her start in coaching, or any enthusiastic yet not necessarily knowledgeable or experienced individual to start out. And enthusiasm is a necessity, because without that trait, those freshmen players aren't going to have as much fun as they should, and at the freshman level, fun is a higher priority than at the other two.

An enthusiastic young coach is also more likely to stick around to help at varsity practices, be on the bench at varsity games (and keep track of timeouts and/or fouls, for example) and help with the scouting. An energetic young coach can also relate to the players, especially a female one, and having someone like that on the staff can be a tremendous asset when the inevitable mood swings occur during the long season.

The junior varsity coach needs more experience and also must be committed to your system and style. It is imperative that she run the same basic offenses and same basic defenses as the varsity and exactly the same inbounds plays and pressbreakers. You want your kids to be immersed in your philosophy from the moment they set foot on campus, and since, for girls, the junior varsity may be the only steppingstone between eighth grade and the varsity, the JVs have to do what you do.

In many areas, the junior varsity coach can sit on the bench during varsity games because the two teams play at the same site, but even then you can't lean on her too much. The JV coach won't be in the locker room with you before the game, because her game will still be going on, and she will inevitably be more focused on her team. That's as it should be, but if you want some serious help, you need at least one coach whose sole job is to be your assistant, and preferably two.

Again, your assistant coaches must be committed to your philosophy, and in an ideal world, will have worked with you for several years so they know your system. It's also a good idea to give assistants areas of responsibility, and actually delegate some authority to them. This not only will keep them more involved, it will also make the players respect them more, and thus listen to them more.

For example, when I worked with one very successful head coach as an assistant, I was completely in charge of defensive matchups, before and during the game. Of course we would talk over the general plan, and maybe once or twice in three years he overruled me, but the girls knew, and I knew, that our defensive matchups came down to me — and that strengthened both my commitment and the girls' respect.

During practice, it's also important to use your assistants wisely. Coaches who have been on their own for many years sometimes find it hard to break down into small groups and let the other coaches teach, but in the long run it's better for everyone. Sure, the freshman coach might not teach the drop step exactly the way you would, but it's not going to be flat wrong, and the players will benefit more from having one coach work with four people than you trying to work with 12. Splitting the team into three or four small skills' groups for 20 minutes a practice is a nice change of pace as well as giving players individual attention they might not otherwise get. Even if there are only two coaches, having one work on inbounds plays at one end while the other does post defense drills at the other utilizes time more efficiently than having half the kids sit around and watch the other half do the drills or run the plays.

During games, it's helpful to give your assistants designated roles. One should always watch the 30-second clock (if you have one in your state), and begin counting down (when you have the ball) with 10 seconds left. Make sure the bench joins in the count so that the players on the court definitely can hear how much time is left. Another job for the assistants is to inform the coach how many fouls each player has — after every call. There's no bigger shock to a head coach than to realize that the whistle with 4:21 left just fouled out her star, when the coach thought she only had three. Most of the time, the head coach will already know, but after every foul after the first, an assistant should make eye contact with the head coach and signal how many fouls that player has. Finally, an assistant should keep track of time outs for both teams.

Some coaches like to meet with their assistants for 10 seconds before stepping into the huddle after a time out call. This makes sense because it gives the players a chance to get some water and take a deep breath or two before being assaulted with information and/or inspiration. (Speaking of which, water girls (or boys) and water bottles are very helpful. Usually water girls can be recruited from families of the players but they need to commit to being at most of the games. It's also critical that every player have her own water bottle because if players share water bottles, they will also share every known rhinovirus. A parent should be assigned to water bottle duty, so that they are picked up after the game, cleaned, refilled and brought to the next game.)

Most of the time, the head coach does all the talking in the huddle, but there's no reason that an assistant can't take some or all of the minute allotted. The exact structure of your timeouts and the use of your assistants is less important than making sure it happens the same way every time. During the pressure of an important game, the players should be able to take some comfort in their timeout routine and know what to expect from the head coach, the assistants and the water girls.

But there's more to the basketball staff than coaches and water girls. Often the head coach is also responsible for getting people to run the scoreboard, the 30-second clock and, most important, keep score. Usually, the people who run the scoreboard and 30-second clock are paid, which makes it easier to round up warm bodies, but the older they are, the better. You don't want a 16-year-old telling the referee whether or not that game-winning shot was released before the horn sounded (remember, the rule book allows the referee to ask the scoreboard operator to make that kind of decision), and you don't want that 16-year-old bearing the brunt of screams from coaches and fans when the clock doesn't start or stop on time.

And speaking of rules, get a rule book before the start of every season, and read it through, from front to back. You may not think the rules about uniforms matter much, but unless you want to start a postseason game with the other team shooting four technical foul shots because you didn't know all the girls' compression shorts had to be the same color, it's wise to know them.

And it's critical in dealing with officials to make sure that you know the rules. Nothing will make a ref less likely to listen than a coach who doesn't know the rules — and when the time comes that you are right, and you need to have some credibility, the refs will just turn away. On the other hand, if they know that you only complain about truly horrible calls, lack of hustle and rules' mistakes, then you've got a chance to get your point across late in a crucial game.

And speaking of your officials, tell your girls to always be as nice as they can. Let the coaches be the jerks; the girls should be as polite as possible. I even like our players to thank the ref when he hands them the ball at the free-throw line — his attitude toward our team is incredibly important, and I want to take advantage of every opportunity to influence him, especially since you will see the same refs over and over again during the season.

Another important staff member is the scorekeeper, because she will travel with you — and is your only recourse should there be a dispute over the number of fouls, or the score of the game. Ideally, your permanent scorekeeper is an adult who knows the game and is willing to commit to every game. (If you travel long distances, this becomes more problematic, but tournaments have slightly better scorekeepers than usual, so there are fewer problems.) If you are forced to use a student as your scorekeeper, make sure to tell her to be as strong and forceful as she can when dealing with the other team's scorekeeper and the officials. If she immediately backs down, all of a sudden one of your starters may wind up with three fouls when she's only committed two.

Staff concerns don't end at the bench. Often teams are allowed to run the concession stands at home games, which can be a major source of revenue, and sometimes teams are even allowed to keep the gate for their programs during preseason. The head coach should make sure that some-one is handling the staffing for the door and arranging to sell hot dogs, sodas and pizza (get a restaraunt to deliver and mark it way, way up). Not only will you make money off the fans during that game, they will be more willing to come back if they know they can get something to eat and drink.

Finally, and perhaps most critical of all, you must deal with the staff of the school itself. Usually, there are two administrators you must interact with on a regular basis: the principal and the athletic director — but they may not be the most important. Still, we'll deal with them first because they have the most say about your program and your success.

Most of the time, the principal and athletic director want you to succeed, but they sometimes don't understand what success entails. If you win a lot of games at a school where 10 wins was previously cause for celebration, you'll draw bigger crowds — and now the principal has to deal with crowd control, something he never had to do before. And the athletic director may find that he has to field more phone calls and handle more requests for schedules and information from fans and college coaches. Should you begin playing in postseason on a regular basis, the workload for the AD and the principal (and/or vice-principals) also increases. Practice time for spring sports in the gym may be affected by your extended season, which requires juggling and soothing of coachly egos, and administrators will also have to sell tickets, go to meetings and attend events that they may have never had to sell, go to or attend before.

Sometimes, this results in subliminal resentment that can surface as complaints about other issues, but it will pass in time. The rewards of success eventually offset any extra administrative headaches, and as everyone gets used to your new, and more successful, regime, they will make the necessary adjustments so that everything runs relatively smoothly. It's important not to push too hard in the first years, unless as a girls' coach, you feel there is a gender-related agenda at work (there are still the odd antediluvians about who feel that women and girls should only cook, clean and mend). In the majority of cases, though, any resistance you meet is institutional and not intentional — and the best response is to turneth away wrath with a soft word, and fill out every form in triplicate at least two weeks early. (Of course, during your first years there will be times you don't know about forms, or forget to fill them out. You too will make mistakes, and if you're forgiving of the administration's errors, they'll be a lot more lenient with yours in turn.)

There are two other key people that you must develop a solid working relationship with. The first is the principal's secretary, or the school's office manager, depending on the title. The second is the head custodian.

The principal's secretary is the gatekeeper to the principal and spends more time with the school's leader than anyone else. The secretary's opinion of you will be obvious to the principal, and to the rest of the staff, and if it's a bad one, everything you try to do will be harder. Treat the gatekeeper with respect, and if asked to fill out a form by a certain date, make sure you do. It's guaranteed that there will come a time when you will need a favor from the secretary, and you don't want the answer to be no.

The head custodian and the janitorial staff are crucial because there will inevitably be days when the baskets don't come down, or the bleachers are left out after a rally, or they've changed the locks on the circuit-breaker box and you can't turn the lights on. The custodians also will be there for your games and events, and the better job they do, the happier the fans will be, and the better the atmosphere. And every once in a while, just to test you, the school district will change the locks on Friday, so when you come in for your Saturday practice, no key in your possession will work. At that point, you need to be able to call the head custodian and ask for a big favor, because the head custodian may be the only person in the district with the keys you need.

There are actually some other people who are important — the trainer, for example, if your school has one, and the director of the school play, if she needs to use your practice facilities for her shows — but this chapter on staffing has ranged far enough.

And you thought all you had to worry about was the players and the parents.

Chapter 4
Scheduling for Success

Basketball. You remember, the sport with the round ball and the orange rims.

So far, though, we haven't come near a court, and we've got one more chapter to go before we get there — but at least we'll be talking about games and practices for the next thousand words or so.

Yes, it's time to delve into the complexities of the schedule, which is bounded on one hand by your league commitments, and on the other by the needs of your team. There are, of course, many other factors, such as the availability of your gym for home games during preseason, state rules and money for travel, but those are the two most important.

To begin with, your league has committed you to a certain number of games. In some areas, it might be as few as six; in others, it's possible that your entire schedule is locked in. The number of games left over after your league commitments are complete is a crucial component of your schedule and your plans for the team.

In most states, there is a maximum number of games and scrimmages any school is allowed to schedule. In some states, a tournament will be counted as one or two games regardless of how many games are actually played; in others, every game counts as a game, tournament or not; and there are places where the definition of 'tournament' is not what you'd expect. So the first step is to find out the rules that apply to your school, and preferably get them in writing. Every year, it seems, a prominent school gets nailed for playing too many games.

It's also important to know the difference between a game and a scrimmage. In some states, you can't keep score or even operate the scoreboard during a scrimmage. In others, they can be completely game-like. Make sure you know the rules, because the more successful you get, the more opposing coaches and boosters will start to examine your every move. (And don't think you're safe within the school: If you cut a player whose father thinks she's a basketball goddess, he'll be out to get you — and if he can nab you for a rules' violation, rest assured he will.)

The next level of administrative restraint involves travel. Sometimes, you have to get school board permission to travel out of state, or even out of your district. There's nothing more disconcerting than arranging to play in a tournament in April, and then being told three days before the first game in December that the school board hasn't officially approved the trip — and so you can't go. Some states, in fact, don't allow any team to leave the state, while others set a limit on how far away from home you can go. Other rules that can trip up the best-laid preseason plans involve how many games can played in a row, or how many games in a day (there are tournaments that play two a day), or whether Sunday games are allowed. Again, it's crucial that you know all these rules before you schedule, because usually the bureaucrats won't let you know there's a problem until the very last minute, when it's often too late to solve it. And expect no administrative mercy from the school district or state high school associations. For them, it's by the book or bye-bye.

With all that hassle, you might be tempted not to travel

at all. After all, it's expensive for the players and parents to take a weekend trip to a tournament and stay in motels and eat in restaurants. (Surprisingly, it's not necessarily that much more expensive to travel to an out-of-state tournament than an in-state one. Sometimes the bigger tournaments will give you deals on hotels and meals that will offset the extra travel cost. The biggest expense is the three or four days of lodging and food, not the cost of getting there.) But there are few things that bring a team together more than traveling to an unfamiliar city to play in unfamiliar gyms before crowds that don't even care who you are. In a very real sense, it's your team against the world, and the bonding that occurs in those situations simply can't be duplicated.

My favorite travel story came when we went to Winslow, Ariz., to play before Christmas. I was coaching at Campolindo High School at the time, which is a pretty much all-white school from a very upscale area in Northern California. Winslow, on the other hand, is on a Navajo reservation basically in the middle of nowhere.

Now, for whatever reason, basketball is hugely popular in that area, and there were several mostly Native American teams in this tournament, including the host. We were very good that year and made it to the finals, against the home team. One of the parents asked me what our chances were, clearly expecting me to say 'Oh, we should win.' Instead, I said 'We've got about one chance in four.' She was stunned and naturally asked why. 'Well, they'll foul Tracy (our 6-2 sophomore who later went on to West Coast Conference Player of the Year) out early, and we won't get a call all night.'

And sure enough, that's exactly what happened. In addition, it happened in a packed gym with 900 Navajo and only about 25 Northern Californians, including the players. But the refs lost their concentration in the second half, and we stormed back from 13 down to tie the game and send it into overtime. At that point, the whistles worked again, and we lost by five or six.

After the game, people came up to us and said things like 'You were the better team,' or 'No one ever wins here,' or 'They never lose at home.' Finally, one old Navajo put his arm around me and said, 'Now you know how Custer felt.'

But despite the loss, that was a great experience for our team. We were much better for the games we had played in a hostile environment, and we were much closer because of the time we spent together. And of course, no trip we would take that year would be anywhere near as daunting.

So if you expect to play in postseason and travel outside your immediate area to do so, it is imperative that you travel in preseason. The players, coaches and parents need to know what to expect, and how to handle themselves in terms of getting enough rest and the right kinds of food, and they won't learn how unless they do it. (Speaking of rest, if you can afford it, it's always a good idea to have two players to a room rather than three or four. There's a chance that the players will get enough sleep two to a room — with four, it's almost a guarantee that no one will get enough rest.)

So definitely schedule a road trip, even if it's just a hundred miles away, so that the team has to stay in a motel. If finances are a problem for some kids, well, that's what fundraisers are for. Ideally, the entire trip will be paid for out of team funds so that there's no division between members of the team. After all, the primary virtue of traveling to a tournament is team bonding, and you don't want to put any roadblocks in the way of reaching that goal.

The next step is who to schedule — and that depends a great deal on the makeup of your team and your goals for the season.

Let's begin with a .500 team that's looking to build some momentum. It makes no sense to go out and schedule the best teams and play in a monster tournament if you want to build confidence in your players and your system. In short, you need to schedule some wins, and that means finding some fish in the local pond that you know you can beat. Of course, you also have to schedule some challenging games as well so the team will have something to measure itself against.

For a young team or a team that needs to develop some confidence, my ideal schedule runs something like this: An opening fish that's an easy win; a team at about the same level as we are; and then a very good team. Presumably the first win gives everybody a chance to play after the long weeks of practice and gets the kinks out. The second game is a test of the system and will show some weaknesses that need to be worked on. And a big win can be tempered by the looming specter of the very good team that's next up, so no one can get too cocky.

Getting thumped by a very good team, after a win and a close game, can be a positive. Good teams punish every mistake, and coaches who schedule nothing but fish in preseason will find that their teams get away with too many mistakes and will continue to make them when they face quality opposition. You don't want to wait too long before introducing your team to the level of play you want them to reach, and visiting the gym of one of the best teams in your area and allowing your players to absorb the atmosphere and attitude of a top program is a very good thing — even if you have to absorb a 25-point loss at the same time.

And naturally, you'd like to follow that game against the local power with another fish, so everyone can get their confidence back. If you have enough games on your schedule, it's wise to play a tournament that doesn't require travel, to get the team used to playing several games in a short span of time, since often postseason play demands the same. Then go away for a pre-Christmas tournament, come back with a fish in the week after Christmas and roll into league with a wide variety of experiences under your collective belt.

Obviously, different teams will have different goals. If you have a state title contender in hand, you need to go to war as often as possible so your players are ready for anything. On the other hand, if postseason seedings and possible home games are determined by overall record or some kind of power rating, you must be very aware of exactly what criteria are used to determine your seeding. It may be that, in some states, the best road to a championship is to amass as many wins as possible, and thus get as many postseason home games as possible.

Regardless, crafting your schedule is a key component in a team's success. For example, some strong teams play in very weak leagues, so they get lazy and sloppy in January and February because of too many blowouts. Those teams should look for the Martin Luther King Day shootouts that have sprung up around the country or should try to schedule Saturday games with other strong teams to try and stay sharp. Going 16-0 in a league that required you to play just four tough games won't get you ready for postseason play.

And don't forget that, as varsity coach, you also have to schedule your junior varsity and freshman games (unless you're lucky enough to have an active athletic director who'll take care of that for you). Try to get both teams into at least one tournament, though neither needs to travel.

It's also important to make sure that if you travel to a nearby powerhouse one year that the favor is returned the next. Some states require signed contracts, which makes it easy, but if it's just coach-to-coach, make sure to put that home-and-home concept out there early in the conversation. Some coaches will still back out, but most will stick to their original agreement. Still, though, if it's never mentioned at all, don't assume that you'll get a return visit.

OK, now you've got your schedule — but how are you going to give your team the best chance to win against your opponents? One key component of the answer is scouting.

Some teams have elaborate scouting reports, breaking down an opponent into offense, defense, press/pressbreaker, inbounds plays and individual tendencies, and naturally the more information the better. Sure, some players won't absorb much, but some will, and it can be a huge difference if your point guard knows the other point guard only goes left and can take that away.

But even if all you know is that your upcoming opponent plays a 2-3 zone, has two three-point shooters, likes to run and has a foul-prone center, you can prepare your team much more effectively. Unfortunately, the only way you can ensure that you will have even this kind of rudimentary scouting report is if you send someone to see the team play. In an ideal world, there's a local fan who loves the game and is willing to drive to out-of-the-way gyms and take copious notes that she will then turn into a neatly typed scouting report. More likely, you or your staff will have to do a lot of it, or you'll have to send someone out with a camcorder to bring you back a tape.

Regardless, though, it needs to be done. After all the work you and your players have put in, it is dangerous to give away the first quarter while you try to figure out what the other team has. Maybe that 6-3 girl shoots threes. Maybe that weird zone is a matchup. Maybe they play an unusual halfcourt trap. And if you think you can communicate just how to handle that 1-3-1 trap during a timeout, you're dreaming — and by the time you get into the locker room at half you could be down 15 to an inferior team because you didn't know what they were going to do. And even the 10 minutes at halftime isn't going to really help your players break down something they've never seen before. Spending 10 minutes on it at practice the day before the game, though, will prepare everyone for what's coming, and then adjustments are much easier to make.

So think about scouting, and get the schedule of every team you're going to play. Sometimes that will take several phone calls to coaches and athletic directors, but it's well worth the hassle. (In a tournament, you only need to do advance scouting for the first opponent; but make sure that you're getting tape or a scouting report from the game matching your possible opponents once you get there.)

Once you have your opponents' schedules, sit down and figure out when and where you're going to see the top teams you'll be playing. You don't need to know much about the doormat in your league that you expect to beat by 30 — but make sure and pay attention to all the pre-season scores to see if they've improved. Generally, you'll want scouting reports on at least half the teams you play, and, depending on how serious you are, about two-thirds. And if you send someone out to videotape, they need to return with a program that lists the heights and classes of the opposing players (once we got a report off a tape that a team had three 5-10 girls and a bunch of 5-7 players, but it turned out they were 5-8 and 5-4, respectively, which created some matchup problems we didn't expect). It's also critical that the taper talk into the microphone during the game, saying the number of the player with the ball. Given the lighting in many gyms, and the resolution of the tape, it's often impossible to tell one dark-haired ponytailed player from another, and you'll be looking at the screen from two inches away trying to figure out whether it was 24 or 12 who hit that three from the corner.

And it will be a worthwhile investment to get a good VCR, one with a good remote control that starts and stops the action quickly, and preferably one that can play camcorder tapes as well as VCRs. You'll be amazed how much quality time you'll spend in front of it.

The last scheduling item is practice. If you're lucky, the athletic director takes care of this whole problem, and shows no bias toward any team. Sometimes, though, it's up to the coaches of the basketball and wrestling teams to hammer out some kind of arrangement, which can turn into a contentious process. Regardless of who makes the schedule, every coach should have a copy in writing, so that when two teams show up at the same time, there's something to refer to. A meeting early in the fall to iron out practice scheduling issues (such as the JV coach who can't practice before 7 p.m., or the freshman boys' tournament that will eat up the gym for an entire weekend) is a very good idea, even if the AD does all the dirty work. The more input the better, or you could wind up with a regular 7 a.m. slot every Saturday.

And now, at last, you're ready to pick up a basketball.

Chapter 5
Practice, Practice, Practice

Two things:
1. What you practice is what you're good at.
2. There's never enough time to practice all the things you want to be good at.

Sure, some states allow teams to practice year-round — but there's still not enough time to instill solid fundamentals in all aspects of the game, get in plenty of shooting, play lots of games (either against other teams or each other) and teach team concepts at both ends of the court. But in most states, where practice time is limited by season of sport, hard choices have to be made.

So step one is to prioritize: What are the most important things you want your team to be able to do? Once you've made that decision, or set of decisions, you can start to organize your preseason and your practices. But don't try to do too much. It's better to be good at just a few things than mediocre at a lot of them.

As an example, a young coach took over one of our neighboring schools several years ago, and it was clear he had just gone out and stripped a local bookstore of books on coaching. His team ran three different zones, two different presses and a myriad of offenses. After I scouted them for a half, I quit writing, because two things had become clear: 1) Our kids would never manage to absorb everything he had installed, and 2) neither would theirs.

Over time, the young coach matured, as young coaches

do, and he had his players do fewer and fewer things. Not surprisingly, they did them better and better, and now the program is one of the best in the area.

As for specific drills, there are plenty of books and videos with hundreds of excellent drills, so don't look for them here. Instead, we'll talk about the bigger picture and how and when you'll fit those drills that you and your players like into the limited time that you have. And, as usual, we'll start at the very beginning.

So the season's just ended. After a couple of weeks off, you'll be ready to go, and if you're a new head coach, there's nothing you'd like better than to start installing your system. But very few states allow you to practice in the spring, and the softball and track coaches probably have some other things in mind for your players. That doesn't mean, however, you can't do anything.

First, the players are tired of practice and maybe even basketball in general after the season. Let them recover for several weeks, and then open the gym and roll out the balls. There's no need to coach at this point — just let the kids have fun playing the game. Keep the boys out, if possible, and have twice weekly open gyms (Sunday evenings are a great time) for about 90 minutes. There should be minimal structure, and the goal should be for players to run up and down, try things they haven't tried before, adjust to their new roles and, most important, enjoy the game.

In my opinion, many girls don't play the game as often as boys do. They don't go down to the playground and play three-on-three, so the opportunity to just get in some games is of greater value for girls than boys. It's also vital to keep score, as on the playground, so that the kids start to understand game strategy and develop a competitive edge.

Some instruction can take place: Pulling a player aside after a pickup game and telling her she needed to go to the basket on that last fast break or to look for the three when her team needs a bomb to win is worthwhile. But too much coaching takes the fun out of it. One thing, though — do the matchups yourself. The kids will tend to guard their friends or the people they always guard, and they'll get a little lazy. Force the posts to guard perimeter players; make the freshman try and stay with the star; put the three-point shooter on a smaller player and ask her to post up.

It's also a good idea to bring in some older players, male and female. Mix the veterans in (the junior varsity coach, an assistant or even you, if you're up for admitting your own mistakes and tarnishing your image as a perfect player) and let the oldsters push, shove and use all the tricks they've learned. It's especially good for girls to learn that it's not OK for older men to push them around. In relationships, at work and on the basketball court, it's crucial for young women to learn that they must stand up to males who try to dominate them. Maybe the guy will be stronger (or richer or whatever), but the girl still must try and stand up for herself. (Make sure the older guys especially understand their roles. They shouldn't block every shot they can, but if a girl makes a mistake, then a blocked shot is OK. And the guys should use their quickness at every opportunity but hold back on using their strength, since it's unlikely the girls will see opponents as strong as men, but they might see some who are just as quick.)

Some coaches prefer playing in a spring (or fall) league to open gyms, but we like the freeform situation of open gyms. It's more fun (and fun often gets left behind in serious programs) and it also allows girls to try new things. Seldom will a player show off a new move in a game with refs, fans in the stands and players from opposing schools, but she just might in an open gym when she's guarded by an eighth grader. It takes time and patience to develop new skills, and organized games don't encourage creativity or experimentation.

Once school is out, the intensity should go up a notch. After all, the sport a young athlete plays in the summer is the one she's most serious about. Some may try to play two during the vacation, but since tournaments in all sports are on the weekends, conflicts will inevitably arise. It's unfair in a way, but in the summer, athletes have to make a choice: Am I going to play club volleyball or summer basketball? Am I going to play basketball every weekend or swim?

This is a delicate situation, because you don't want to put too much pressure on youngsters, but on the other hand you want the best athletes in the school to play your sport. And it's true that the players who are on the summer team are going to be the ones most likely to be on the varsity in November, both because they've made the commitment, and because they've also improved the most. It's a truism that players get better in the offseason and then apply that improvement during the season, and you'll find that the great athlete who plays volleyball in the summer will be passed in basketball effectiveness by the good athlete who only plays hoops.

But the summer equation is not a simple one. Once you get players to commit to basketball, you'll discover that some are being recruited by AAU teams — and those teams offer a higher level of competition, travel and more exposure to college coaches and scouting services. Only your stars will be recruited, but since your stars are the key to your success, you naturally want them to play in your system and with your team rather than some other coach and a bunch of talented strangers. Here, however, is where you'll show your true colors to the players. If you insist that a player retard her development and limit her college options by playing with the high school team in the summer, you'll get a deserved reputation as a selfish coach.

What you have to do here is bite the bullet and try to compromise. Work it out so that your star can play some summer league games and some tournaments with the high school team, while getting the most for her AAU dollars. Try to make it easy for her to do both, and don't make her feel guilty for not playing solely with the high school team. And if she winds up not playing with you at all, well, look at it this way: Your lesser players will improve more because they'll get more playing time, so your depth will be better come the season.

Of course, you can form your own AAU team. That's been the ticket to success at Narbonne, the dominant high school team in the nation in the late '90s and right after the turn of the century. James Anderson and his father made their AAU club team a Narbonne team, and even though they sometimes got beat playing against the other AAU teams, which are mostly all-stars, it still honed and developed the players in the Gaucho system.

Few high schools, however, will have the level of talent that's available to a Los Angeles school, and so an AAU campaign could prove to be nothing but a series of bad, frustrating losses. And if you mix in stars from other teams with your players to be competitive, you won't be preparing your girls for the roles they'll play during the season. Still, in some situations, a high school coach should carefully consider forming her own AAU team and going out on the circuit with the big stars and the college coaches. If everyone can keep her head up, the experience can be invaluable.

Another issue is who's on that summer team. You may know who you want on next year's varsity by April 1, but most districts prefer the fiction that there are open tryouts in November and every kid in the school has a chance to make the team. (Of course if a 6-5 foreign exchange student from Lithuania ducks through the doorway Sept.

15, you're going to find room, but 90% of the time you know who will be on the team long before the first day of practice.) So if there are borderline players, or kids who think they are borderline players, they must have a chance to play with the varsity during the summer. Ideally, you'll have two or even three separate teams playing at the same time, and since people will inevitably be missing from the varsity at one point or another, you can rotate borderline players up to the top team so they have a chance to show what they can do at that level.

It's expensive, of course, to have summer teams, and parents are going to have to pay as much as $350 for the summer schedule. Again, in an ideal situation, team fundraising will have paid the freight, but there's no escaping the fact that summer basketball costs money. You should play in one or two leagues and try to schedule at least four tournaments between the middle of June and August 1. (I like to give everyone a week off around July 4 and be done by August. That gives families — and coaches — the July 4 window and all of August to schedule vacations.) If the junior varsity summer team is going to play fewer games, the price can be lower, but money will be an issue. The more that can come from team funds the better, for even if there's extra money to offset costs for poorer families, pride can get in the way. It's very hard for many people to ask for charity, and it's also difficult, once a family has accepted money from the team, for that family to feel good about going out to dinner on a road trip or to have anyone else see them spending money on even little luxuries.

There should be no more than 12 people on each team (some programs have as many as four) so that there's plenty of playing time to go around — and of course everyone should play in the summer. Sometimes coaches will allow everyone to play equal amounts of minutes all summer, but there is another side to the story. Some players, usually your best ones, can get annoyed if they wind up losing to a rival who plays the starters the whole game rather than rotates players, so be aware of people's feelings on the issue. Sometimes you might play everyone in the first half and then go for the win in the second half by running out only your best. Regardless, though, everyone has to play a substantial amount if everyone's paying. (Money, as Lauryn Hill once pointed out, changes the situation.)

It also might be a good idea to finish the summer season with a pool party or group outing to a WNBA or major league baseball game. It's a long road through July, and a celebration can be a lot of fun for everyone.

A second summer necessity is a skills camp. We like to run a three-week, two-hour-a-day camp for all the returners, incoming freshmen and outstanding junior high players. This camp is almost totally devoted to ballhandling, rebounding, fundamentals, defense and shooting. You will probably have no more than 40 kids, who should be divided into four groups of roughly equal ability. Ideally, the head coach won't run a teaching station, which means four coaches/former players should be on hand. A two-hour session should begin with 10 minutes of socializing (a special necessity for girls), followed by four 20-minute stations and concluding with 30 minutes of scrimmaging.

Again, this will cost money (unless you get your high school gym time for free), but if players are serious about basketball they must come to the camp. Those who don't are going to fall behind, just as those who don't play in the summer leagues will. Camp and the summer team are necessities for long-term success, and no team without them is going to achieve elite status.

Once school starts, it's back to open gyms. Some coaches do heavy conditioning work in the fall (and sometimes that's all they can do), but we'd rather have the kids playing the game. The benefits of weight-lifting evaporate unless an in-season program is installed, and there's usually not time for school, practice, games and weights once the real season begins. And September sprints don't have much carryover value in February. In fact, we've found that kids who come out after volleyball (which is generally two weeks after basketball practice has started), and not in particularly good shape, catch up more rapidly than you'd think. They are 16, after all, and the body functions quite well at that age, so, by mid-December, you'll be hard-pressed to pick out the kids who were there from day one from the kids who came late. And by March, when it really counts, fall conditioning has no impact at all. So we'd rather have them play the game, because the benefits of playing are much greater than the benefits of running and lifting weights.

The next big moment is tryouts. Some districts have separate tryouts, while others expect tryouts to take place during the limited practice time available. Either way, you don't want to waste too much time on tryouts since you've had spring, summer and fall to evaluate most of your talent. A couple of players might still be on the bubble, but you don't want to string anyone along. (And when you cut people, call them or do it face-to-face. None of this posting-the-names-in-the-p.e.-office. Sure cutting people is a horrible job, but if you expect your players to do difficult things, you should do some too.)

In any event, make the cuts quickly and move on. You can allow the junior varsity and freshman coaches to take a longer time (especially the frosh coach, who will have lots of players who are just trying the game out for the first time), but you need to start practicing with your team, and the sooner the better.

Yes, you've had 20 open gyms where the kids have played a lot of fun games where they can try new things. And you've had a summer camp, they gotten a lot of work on fundamentals. If you've played 30 games during the summer, they've begun to bond as a team and started to learn what their roles will be. All of which means you don't have to do any of those things during your precious in-season practice time, which won't ever be enough to do all that you want, and need, to do.

At the risk of being repetitious, I have to mention again that you don't have enough time to do everything well, but you do have time to do some things well. Our program emphasizes defense, and so we spend a lot of time doing defensive drills (just pick the ones you like from the many available). We also are firm believers in the three-pointer, and we have everyone on the team (and we mean everyone) shoot 10 minutes of threes every practice. We like to get some free throws in every practice and lots of shooting (after all, you determine who wins by who puts the ball in the hoop more often). Where we tend to skimp is our half-court offense, for this reason: For the benefits (baskets scored or prevented), practicing complicated offensive maneuvers doesn't help much. Sure, you'll get some easy hoops by running your plays against weaker teams, but the good teams will have you scouted, and you won't get any cheapies.

But you may feel differently, and that's fine too. We'll discuss offensive and defensive philosophies in more detail in later chapters, but the following hard truths cannot be overemphasized: What you practice is what you're good at, and you don't have enough time to be good at everything. If you spend too much time on the half-court set or on shooting threes, you won't be as good on defense or in the last two minutes. It's a matter of setting your priorities, and following through.

And what exactly do you need to do? Let's start with offense ...

Chapter 6
The Fundamentals of Offense

You have to score to win. This isn't soccer and score-less ties are not an option. Even in states without a 30-second clock, there's a premium on putting points on the board — and here's just one reason: An uptempo team that scores in the 60s night in and night out can overcome a shaky start. The players will have confidence that they can erase a 10-point deficit, or higher, because they know they can score. But a team that's happy to win 38-35 will find it hard to overcome a six-point margin in the last three minutes, because six points might be a quarter's output.

So, in general, the ability to score in bunches is a good thing — but if you are a defense-first coach, and the rest of the league has more talent and athleticism than you do on a yearly basis, maybe you'll want to slow the game down and occasionally explode for 50. There's no sense in trying to run with people who will always run faster than you, and if your best chance to win is by limiting athleticism's opportunities to win the game, by all means run some clock on every possession.

Either way, though, you have to have an offense. But first, what does 'offense' mean? Most coaches will auto-matically assume it's the Xs and Os drawn up on the board before the season, but if you really think about it, what percentage of your scoring comes from your set offense?

This is an absolutely key point, because we've already discussed how there's just not enough time to practice everything that needs to be practiced — so if you spend 30 percent of your practice time on an offense that only generates 15 percent of your points, you've got a problem. And now consider how many of your points come off of opponents' turnovers? Or your press? Or after defensive rebounds? Or after offensive rebounds? Or at the free-throw line?

Some of the points generated by offensive rebounds or at the line might be credited to your set offense, but, especially later in the year, that weakside screen just won't create an easy layup any more. (Don't forget to factor in the missed open shots in your offense. They don't count as baskets, and maybe, just maybe, if you'd spent more time shooting in practice instead of running plays, more of those 10-footers would go in.)

The more deliberate your offense, the less you press, the more important your halfcourt offense becomes, because it will generate a higher percentage of your points. But if you're like most teams, you'll run when you can and maybe even when you can't, and so you may discover that your plays don't really do that much for you.

In fact, I would argue that 90 percent of set offenses result, at best, in a situation where one of your players has a chance to go one-on-one against an opponent. If your player is better, then you have a good chance to score; if the other team's player is better, you're in trouble. And that, in a nutshell, is why the better team usually wins. The best an offense can do is set up some one-on-one opportunities, which will only succeed if you have more talent. If you don't have more talent on the floor, it doesn't matter what you run.

Again, though, you have to have an offense — my primary point is that it really doesn't matter which one, as long as you believe in it, you have the players to run it, and you run it well. But any team that has 15 set plays and three different motions is wasting its time. That's not because those 15 plays and three motions don't work, but that the benefit they produce isn't worth the time they take to learn. Teach one continuous motion offense to everyone in your program (preferably one that doesn't require the wing to create a lead every single time) and throw in several set plays that take advantage of your material in a given season, and leave it at that. The rest of the time, work on offensive principles, offensive moves and shooting. And shooting. And more shooting. And then some more shooting.

It doesn't matter how well you run the play if you miss the layup. It doesn't matter how wide open the 10-footer is if no one can make it. And it doesn't matter if you draw the foul if you can't convert at the line.

Since one of my roles has almost always been as a shooting coach, I could go on and on about shooting fundamentals, etc., but there are books and videos that cover that subject more than adequately. But here are two things to remember: 1) You cannot correct a player's form when she's a sophomore. If you can't get to her by sixth or seventh grade to instill proper fundamentals (most important, shooting with the elbow directly under the ball and the elbow at least shoulder-high), changing them after that will only lead to frustration. Habits are hard to break, especially if those habits have managed to get a girl on the varsity. Why should she change what got her here? And, in the heat of a game, she will almost always revert to her old form. 2) Practicing fundamentally unsound shots will not necessarily improve shooting percentage. Since you can't really alter too much about the shot, it's important to make sure that players are at least on balance, don't overstride and do the same thing every time.

But this chapter isn't about shooting, it's about scoring, which of course are two different things. This chapter also isn't about running the play, which is an all-too-common focus of too many players and coaches. The object of the game is to score, not to execute the offense, and far too often players get caught up in making the next programmed pass instead of trying to break down the defense. So here are my three keys to any offense:

1. The first thing any player must do after getting the ball is look at the basket. With depressing regularity, a girl on the perimeter will receive a pass and immediately look in the direction of the next pass. This tendency can do more to kill your halfcourt efficiency than almost any other bad habit — and here's why.

   First, if the player with the ball doesn't look at the basket, her defender will not step out to guard her. Instead, the on-ball defender (in zone or man) will sag off toward the basket, cutting off passing lanes and adding more help to the interior. In addition, other defenders on the perimeter don't have to worry about helping to protect the basket, and thus can play the passing lanes more aggressively. So if the player with the ball doesn't look at the hoop, her defender can help out on other offensive options, and other defenders can shut down the passing lanes.

   But if the player first looks at the hoop, now her defender must respect her, even if she can't shoot very well (and most likely, the opposition has a limited idea of her skills). The defense will almost always take a step up, which opens a passing lane to the block. And remember, high school defenses sometimes make mistakes, and it very well could happen that one of your post players is completely unguarded on the block due to a defensive breakdown — but if the player with the ball never looks at the basket, she won't see her. (This also happens on inbounds plays, which we'll discuss in more detail in a later chapter.)

By looking at the basket and ball-faking in that direction, your player has now made the defense react to her and created openings and passing lanes that weren't there before. By not looking at the basket, your player gives the defense command of the halfcourt, even though you have the ball.

2. The second thing that any player with the ball must do is look to score. This sounds simplistic on the surface, but if you examine your offense, you'll realize that many passes result in players getting the ball with no realistic expectation of scoring — and so they don't even think about it. Their defender could fall in a heap on the ground in front of them, and they would still make the next pass, even if no one was between them and the basket.

Girls must constantly be reminded that the object of the game is to put the ball in the hoop, not run the play. They must always look for a way to score, because that's the goal of any offense. And if you get a layup and don't run the play, isn't it better than running the play and missing a 10-footer?

To get your players to look to score, they need to have confidence in their ability to make a basket, and though obviously the variation in talent at the high school level is wide, every player should have an idea of her best chance to score. That's where practicing shooting comes in — it will hurt a team if one girl is no threat because a well-prepared opponent will simply ignore her. If two players can't score at all except on wide-open layups, the problems mount because now the defense can begin to dictate what the offense can and cannot do.

But remember this: Getting to the foul line is scoring, and players who can do little else but dribble can also be effective offensive players. This conveniently leads me to my next point, which is ...

3. Initiate contact. Some people say football is a contact sport, but they're wrong — football is a collision sport. Basketball is a contact sport, a concept that many girls have trouble embracing. But on the offensive end, and especially on the way to the basket, girls must seek out contact. One of the most common reasons for missed layups is that players will move away from the defender and try to shoot over her. This is a bad tactic for a variety of reasons:

♦ Good shooters need to be either set or moving directly toward the basket to score. Moving sideways through the air almost guarantees a miss, and successful layups almost always result from a direct course to the basket. If a defender happens to be in the way, girls must be taught to go through that defender to the hoop, rather than around her. Sure, you'll get a charge or two, but you'll get a lot more free throws.

♦ Fouls are an incredibly important part of the game, and if you commit fewer fouls than the other team, you are going to win most games. One of the best ways to get fouls called on the opposition is to go hard to the hoop, because officials are more likely to blow their whistles on shot attempts. In addition, those defenders closest to the hoop are usually the other team's tallest players — and if you can get them in foul trouble, you will get them off the court. Finally, drawing shooting fouls means you shoot more free throws because you don't have to be in the bonus to get to the line. So sending a small guard headlong into the lane isn't as dumb as it seems. Some shots will be blocked, granted, but fouls will also be called, and free throws shot.

♦ Basketball is a physical, aggressive sport, and avoiding contact will put your team out of synch with those two basic principles. You need to establish a physical presence on the court, and you always need to be aggressive. Going straight at the basket fulfills both those requirements.

This physicality should also spill over into your motion, which against a man will naturally include lots of screens. Screens must be set with intensity, and it's imperative that the person being screened for make contact with her teammate as she goes by. Girls need to be encouraged to make contact at all times on the court, and never more so than in screening situations. The screener must anticipate, and even relish, the chance to impede a defender, and the player screened for must help her do that by setting up the screen and making shoulder-to-shoulder contact with the screener.

This is especially important in the pick-and-roll, which should be a part of any team's man-to-man offense. There's a reason the pick-and-roll is a staple of offense at every level: It works. Just ask John Stockton and Karl Malone. It's also a very good way to get a quick shot when time is an issue, but it takes some practice to make it work properly. Of course, it works best with a guard who can shoot and pass, and a big player who can screen and convert inside, but if nothing else, it can create mismatches that can be exploited later in the offensive motion.

Other set plays should be installed to:

♦ Get your best three-point shooter (who might be your center) a look at a three in fairly short order.

- Get the ball to the block to exploit a mismatch.
- Get your best mid-range jumpshooter a look from 15-feet.
- Isolate your best one-on-one player on the wing.

Again, it doesn't really matter what these plays are, but they should be a consistent part of your strategic arsenal throughout the program. Yes, teams will have them scouted, but every year you will have slightly different talent, so the plays will vary. For example, most of the time you want to run the pick-and-roll so that the dribbler can go to her right, but you might have a player who's better to her left, so the play that year, or for that girl, will go to the other side.

But not everybody plays man-to-man, and a good zone defense can be the most frustrating defense to attack — for good reason. Against a decent zone, especially one that sags off and dares you to shoot, there's only one cure: Make your shots. If you hit some threes and some jumpers, your zone offense is the product of a brilliant basketball mind. If you can't make a thing outside the paint, your zone offense is the product of a know-nothing bumbler who couldn't plan a two-car parade. Yes, you're running the same pattern both times, but the fans and players won't notice. They'll only see that the scoreboard isn't changing.

There are many ways to attack a zone, but there is one constant: Ball fake. You must have your perimeter players set up almost every pass with a ball fake — or two or three. Strong ball fakes create a problem for a zone defense: If the players react, they are wasting energy and jumping out of position; if they don't react, and it isn't a fake, they are out of position. And, after a while, the defense will be so accustomed to a ball fake before every pass that you can then start passing without faking, and the defense will be slow to respond.

Our favorite zone attack keeps the posts below the zone (near the baseline), has no set movement pattern, relies on the dribble to draw a double-team, and tries to work inside out. And if we have good shooters, it's a pretty good offense. If we don't, it's pretty lame. Your zone attack might keep the posts high, be very structured, and love the skip pass. If you can shoot, this will work like a charm. If not, people will start asking you why you don't dribble into the gaps more.

Finally, a word about the three-point shot. The three-pointer is a tremendous weapon, and not just for its obvious mathematical benefits — its psychological impact is even greater. Fans and players alike get off on the three-pointer, and a couple bombs can completely shift the momentum of the game. In addition, three-point shooters stretch the defense, open up the lane, and allow other players to penetrate or post up. Just like dunks in boys' games, three-pointers are daggers to the heart in girls' games.

Remember this: A 33 percent shooter from three-point distance is as effective as a 50 percent shooter from inside the line — and a 25 percent shooter from beyond the arc is comparable to a 37.5 percent shooter, which is about average or even slightly above average for most high school teams. So even if your best three-point shooter misses seven out of ten, she's still helping you, and they give you a puncher's chance to pull off an upset or a big comeback.

All of which means that you should spend part of your practice time having everyone shoot threes. Everyone. Over the years, we have had huge three-pointers come from post player, who may not be quite as good at it as guards, but they usually get a much better look because the defense sags off. The posts, however, will resist shooting the three at first, as will a lot of players who have trouble dealing with a 70 percent failure rate, which is why we do it for 10 minutes every practice. After the first year, there was a marked improvement. After the second year, we were better still, and the ability of almost all of our players (a few just never get it) to make threes gives us a tremendous weapon.

Case in point: We had one girl who was a four-year varsity player who started her last two seasons. Going into her junior year, I coaxed her to shoot more threes — which she did. Unfortunately, she didn't make any. In fact, she didn't really come close, and eventually quit shooting them at all. At the start of her senior year, I pulled her aside and said, 'Chelsea, I have two goals for you this year: Don't get hurt, and make a three.' Well, she didn't make any threes for the first few weeks, but she started taking them. In January, she finally banked one in, much to the amusement of everyone. But she made a couple more, and then, in a huge game with an archrival, she got an open look late in the game — and capped our comeback by drilling the three (great rotation, nothing but the bottom of the net). It was one of those classic 'No, no, no ... great shot!' moments, but it was also the fruition of four years of shooting threes every day in practice and constant encouragement. And needless to say, the opposing coaches were even more stunned than we were, and you could feel the air go out of the other team.

Our substitutes, too, are shooting 10 minutes of threes every day, which means they have a decent chance to come in and make a three — and there is nothing more devastating to an opponent than when a player they don't even know about hits a three in a close game. You can almost see them wonder, 'How good is this team if she can make a three?'

But of course if your sub doesn't come off the bench looking at the basket and looking to score, you won't get that three, or much of anything else. Offense is a state of mind, not a drawing on the chalkboard, and if you expect to score, you must implant an offensive mindset in your team. Basketball players have to be aggressive, physical and confident to succeed, and your offense, whatever it might be, must encourage your players to develop those attributes.

Chapter 7
Developing a Defense

As important as defense is, when you get right down to it, there's not all that much to say. In fact, you could shrink almost every defensive philosophy to two maxims:
- Protect the basket.
- Stop the ball.

But since I've got a whole chapter to fill here, some more detail is in order.

Clearly, the closer the ball is to the basket, the more damage the offense can do — uncontested layups are both dangerous and demoralizing. So no matter what defensive scheme is in operation, it's imperative to protect the basket. Sometimes that protection might involve a few hard fouls, just to let the other team know there are no free lunches, but it's better to be so organized defensively that the basket is never left unprotected no matter what is going on out on the perimeter.

But to protect the basket, sooner or later you have to stop the ball. The ball, and the person who's holding it must be stopped because obviously the opposition can't score without using the ball to do so.

If you put these two axioms together, you can construct a successful defensive system, whether it be zone or man, press or halfcourt. If you consistently protect the basket and stop the ball, you will be a good defensive team.

But most coaches don't want to construct their own defensive system — they'd rather rely on one that has worked in the past. Well, man-to-man works quite well for some teams. And zone works quite well for other teams. And a lot of teams do both with some flair. Down at the bottom of the standings, though, you'll find those teams that don't play any defense particularly well, so regardless of how many points they score, they still struggle.

So don't look for any answers to the zone-man debate here, except that a good team is nothing if not versatile. I would like my teams to be able to play pressure man-to-man when the situation demands it, sagging man-to-man in rare circumstances, a solid zone to deal with teams that can't shoot, and some halfcourt traps to change the pace (fullcourt presses will be dealt with in the special teams chapter).

More specifically, I like to be able to press man-to-man and double-team aggressively in halfcourt man. My zone of choice is the 2-3, and my halfcourt trapping zone is a 1-3-1. For simplicity's sake, some coaches like to use the same trapping zone and base zone, but that's up to you. What's important is that every defense you run protects the basket and stops the ball.

But I can mentally see some hands raising in the back of the room. 'We're the slowest team in creation; in our league, everybody is quicker. Why should we play man at all?' Good question — but it's my firm belief that players need to learn man-to-man fundamentals to be good zone defenders. The best zones are usually played by teams with players who would also do well in man-to-man because those players are capable of creating havoc. Sitting back in a zone and letting the other team beat itself might be a good strategy during the league season (if you're in a weak league), but come postseason you'll run into teams that will shoot you out of that zone, so you'd better have a plan B.

And this is where the halfcourt zone trap comes in. Let's say you're not quick enough to press fullcourt or play man-to-man. There will still be times you need to either get your kids more aggressive or come up with some steals. A good halfcourt trap is much more about swarming to the ball and anticipating lazy passes than it is about individual athleticism, and it's often true that pressing teams don't handle pressure well because they never see it. When the other coach calls time to diagram the play to break down the trap, you simply switch back to the zone — or go to man-to-man for a sequence or two. One of the best things you can do defensively is to force the other team's guards to think, especially if those guards are quicker than your defenders. If they're thinking, they're not attacking, and if they're not attacking, they're not using their quickness.

The ability to switch defenses can also be a confidence builder when things are going wrong. Sometimes the other team is just hot, and your players are getting demoralized. Sooner or later the other team will cool off, and switching defenses may hasten that time. Even if it doesn't, it gives your players a boost because now they can feel they've got a different way to win.

As for the nuts and bolts of zones and man-to-man, pick your poison. There are tapes and books all over, or you can just call up a local coach with a reputation for playing good defense and pick her brain. Eventually, though, it will come down to a commitment to defense at all levels of your program. It must be clear to every player, no matter how talented or what age, that if they are ever going to play for your varsity, they must play defense first. If offensive stars who are lazy defenders find themselves benched in sixth grade games, they'll get the message — and play defense a little harder. (Allowances must be made for scorers who simply can't defend. As long as they work hard at defense, their deficiencies can be accepted, but the player who simply doesn't care about defense cannot be tolerated.)

There is one defensive style, however, that deserves special mention, and that is the nasty and confusing matchup zone. There are lots of wrinkles in various matchups, but the concept boils down to this: A matchup zone puts constant man pressure on the ball, while playing zone principles in the rest of the court.

That may sound simple, but it is actually incredibly complex. If you closely examine a matchup, you'll notice times when people are sprinting from the three-point line to the block in response to a pass, and that sometimes those sprints seem to make no sense. But though the rules that make the matchup work occasionally lead to odd switches, once mastered, they are very difficult for a high school offense to deal with. The pressure on the ball means that the usual zone attacks don't work because the first thing the guard has to do to make an entry pass is break down the defense — and once that happens, the normal zone attack has disappeared. And man-to-man offenses simply won't work against the matchup, especially because it's such an unfamiliar defense.

The big problem is, not surprisingly, that because it's an unfamiliar defense, it's hard to teach and hard to learn, and teams that play it must play it almost all the time. If they make the commitment, though, and struggle through the early confusion, a high school team with a solid grasp of the matchup zone will confuse and frustrate even the most talented opponents.

This leads to another consideration for defenses: If you only play man-to-man, how will your team learn to handle zones? In practice, you can always shred that bad zone your players attempt, but come league season, all those easy hoops that you get against your own kids stumbling around in a 1-2-2 just won't happen. And if you only play the matchup, how will you practice against a man or 2-3 zone?

The flip side of that argument is also important. If you constantly run the same offensive patterns against your defense in practice, man or zone, the defense will adjust and anticipate — which means when another team does something radically different than what you do, it will be hard to adjust. That's one of reasons I love a freelance, rule-based offense because it doubles your practice efficiency. Every time you're practicing the offense, you're practicing defense too, because no one know exactly what is going to happen next. Which, of course, is what's it like in games.

There is one catch that has yet to be mentioned: You can play the best defense in the world and force a lot of missed shots — but if you don't get the rebound, all that defense doesn't mean a thing. So let's revisit a famous cliché: Offense wins fans, defense wins games and rebounding wins championships.

If you're going to be an outstanding team, you must rebound. And though rebounding is definitely aided by size and jumping ability, it is primarily a result of positioning and relentless hard work. Players must screen out all the time, in every drill, and they must screen out every time. It is absolutely imperative that you put a body on every defender, regardless of how far away they are from the basket, and even then you'll give up some offensive rebounds. An offensive rebound with no defender in contact with the rebounder is the first step on the road to defeat. Rebounding is absolutely critical, and it must be emphasized at every level, before every game and during every practice.

There are some things that can be done to help your players rebound beyond just the fundamentals. The first is to point out that most shots are long, and thus most rebounds land on the opposite side of the basket from the shooter. It is therefore necessary to create lots of space on the weakside block when screening out, and it's also a great idea to head to the weak side when the shot goes up.

Another important rule for rebounders: Don't watch the ball. Once the shot goes up, defenders should look around and find someone to block out (preferably their man). Once they've gotten position, they should then, and only then, look at the basket with their hands up. There's no need to watch the ball the whole way to get a rebound — what matters is having position.

On the offensive side, only one person should not be rebounding, and that's the deep defender. She should call out 'Deep' for two reasons: 1) To make sure someone is deep; and 2) to let everyone else know they should crash the boards. Too often, players more than 15 feet from the basket will not go after rebounds, but if you think about it, they are the most difficult to get a body on. They can pick a path to the hoop and it's very hard for defenders to slow them down. (A team rule: If the word 'deep' does not come out of your mouth, you should be crashing the boards.)

Which leads to another key point: Offensive rebounders shouldn't worry about the ball at all. Once the shot goes up, they should look at the defenders and try to weave their way around them to a good rebounding position near the basket. It doesn't matter where, because the goal is merely to establish good enough position so that if the ball bounces to that area, that player will get the rebound. Don't try to guess where the ball will go; instead, go somewhere close to the basket and grab any rebound that comes near you. Sure it won't work all the time, and you'll often have great position when the ball bounces to the other side — but you will get all the rebounds that come to your area. If, on the other hand, you wait on the perimeter until you see where the ball is going to bounce, you will only get a rebound if everyone else falls down.

This is very counterintuitive, but it is also very effective. Guards especially should use this technique to get good position for rebounds, because even if they don't get the ball, they might draw an over-the-back call if they have established themselves inside a bigger player.

One of the difficulties in practicing rebounding and practicing defense is that it can't be broken down as easily into component parts as shooting or ballhandling. And those drills that do exist can get repetitive. Finally, if you instill too much aggression into practice, you'll wind up beating up your own team.

So defense and rebounding are more about attitude than a particular practice regimen. They must be well known as the keys to your program, and they must be preached, over and over again, until everyone is sick of hearing the words. At that point, repeat them.

You can never be too rich, force too many missed shots or get too many rebounds. Sometimes, clichés are clichés because they're true, and that's the case when it comes to defense and rebounding. Offense is fun, but if you want to have a championship banner hanging up in the gym, defense and rebounding are what will get you one.

Chapter 8
The Care and Feeding of Student-Athletes

It's been fun spending all this time on the basketball court, but a successful program depends on a lot more than the time devoted to the game.

To begin with, your players have to be eligible to play and practice, and that means they, and you, must pay attention to academics. There's nothing more devastating to a team than to lose a couple of players midway through the season because they couldn't keep up in the classroom — or more likely, wouldn't keep up in the classroom.

The first step, as always, is to find out what the rules are. Does your school or league require a minimum gradepoint, or will one F disqualify a player? Is there an appeal process? Can an academic ineligibility be made up before the next quarter's grades are reported? Can an incomplete be given instead of a D or an F? Are progress reports (or midterms or any other number of euphemisms) handed out? If so, will you see them? Will the athletic director?

You cannot rely on players to tell you that they are struggling in class. We have been lucky in having smart kids on our teams, but you never can tell when someone will find themselves teetering on the brink of ineligibility — and if you don't know that the balancing act is going on, you won't be able to help.

So ask. Find out what every kid's gradepoint was the year before. Obviously, you don't have to worry too much about the 3.0 students, but if a player is hovering around 2.0, and 1.7 is ineligible, some extra attention may be called for. Most schools have counselors, and each player would be assigned to a particular counselor, so it's a good idea to make some connection (or have one of your staff make the connection) with the counselor for a borderline student. Find out what classes the player is taking and which ones are the hardest. Talk to the teachers, talk to the parents and, yes, talk to the student — but remember, the player isn't going to tell you what you need to know to avoid ineligibility.

If you have a few players with academic problems, it might be a good idea to set up a study hall, or assign smarter players as academic mentors to the ones who are struggling. (It's important to remember that a passing grade at the high school level usually only takes two things: An honest effort and showing up to class every day. Sure, honors physics is hard, but usually the kids taking that course are in no danger of losing eligibility.)

Find a way to first determine who the problem students are, and then monitor and assist them. That's what school is for, after all.

On another level entirely, you also need to pay attention to the grades, test scores and administrative aspects of players who are going to try to play in college. No matter what the level of the player, be it Division I or Division III, she should take the SAT or ACT at the earliest possible time. This accomplishes two things: 1) If she gets a qualifying score, she has something to show the coach of schools she's interested in attending; and 2) if she doesn't get the score she needs or wants, she still has multiple opportunities to improve with retesting.

There are also NCAA guidelines about submitting

transcripts that must be followed, and those guidelines change with stunning regularity. The NCAA is, overall, a horrid organization more devoted to its silly rules than helping young people, so expect no forgiveness if a 't' is left uncrossed. If possible, contact the NCAA for information regarding its requirements and recruiting rules, though that's no guarantee they'll send anything. I've been waiting for two years.

There is another important aspect of keeping your players on the floor, though, and that's health.

The first part is obvious. Make sure players get enough sleep, which will keep them from getting sick. Adolescents need more sleep than adults, so those early morning weekend practices are more than just an annoyance — they could weaken your players, who will be operating without enough rest pretty much all season. And besides, do you ever play a game at 9 a.m.? It's good to have kids used to exerting themselves at different times of day, but 1 p.m. is the earliest you'd ever play, and it's the earliest you ever need to practice.

Let them sleep. It will make them happier and healthier.

Teenagers also need to think about their diets. For most players, that means not subsisting entirely on burgers, fries and Coke, but for some girls, it means eating at all. Anorexia is a serious problem for female athletes and Shea Ralph, the former UConn star, struggled with it throughout her career. Girls' coaches should keep an eye out for a player who loses muscle mass and doesn't eat much at team gatherings.

In general, though, the most important thing about eating is to make sure that players understand how their bodies digest food. They can't expect to play well if, by the time the game ends, they haven't eaten in eight hours, nor can they expect to play well if they downed a couple chili dogs on the way to the gym.

Common sense is the key here. Players should eat a good meal about 3½ hours before tipoff (depending on individual metabolisms). Pasta is always good, but carboloading and all that other nutritional mumbojumbo really doesn't make nearly as much difference as just getting some solid food in and partway through the system before game time. Pregame pasta feeds (at 4 p.m. for a 7:30 p.m. game) are a good team activity, for not only does it guarantee that the players will at least have the opportunity to eat right, but spending this time together can also helps them focus on the task at hand.

Long drives to games can make this kind of scheduling a bit tricky, however, as can taking the bus with other teams. If the team bus leaves right after school, but the varsity doesn't play until 7:30 p.m., food is a major issue. Having the kids eat hot dogs and candy from the concession stand will not improve your chances of winning, so it might be a good idea to gather up the varsity on arrival and head out to a sandwich shop. Things get more complicated if your team plays at 6 p.m., say, and the bus arrives at 4. Ideally, you'd have the bus leave school earlier, and then stop along the way, but if that can't happen, get some sandwiches and fruit juice and feed everyone while you're riding.

Just make sure you and the players always think about when and what they're going to eat prior to a game. It can make all the difference in the world, especially in that second overtime.

And finally, while we're on the subject of the human body, what about weight training? The football team is at it religiously during the offseason, and so are more and more athletes in other sports. There's no doubt weight lifting will make your players stronger and less likely to be injured, but that assumes two things: 1) That they lift under supervision, at least part of the time; and 2) that they continue to lift during the season.

All the advantages gained by offseason weight-lifting will disappear within a few weeks if the players don't get into the weight room at least once a week during the season. It doesn't have to be a heavy workout, but it needs to be supervised and it needs to be scheduled. Unfortunately, there's never enough time during the season to do homework, play basketball, sleep, go to school and eat, so adding anything else to the mix is a problem. But if you're going to insist that your players lift in the offseason, the lifting must continue during the season, even at the expense of some of your precious practice time.

Weight training is tremendously valuable physically and mentally and has clear and obvious benefits. So does shooting free throws for two hours a day, but who has the time for that? If, however, you're willing to allot an hour a week to maintenance weight training, seriously consider adding offseason lifting to your team's regimen.

It's too easy to focus just on what's happening on the court and forget to keep track of how the kids are doing in class or what they're eating before the games. But these and other offcourt activities have a direct impact on who plays and how well they play, so ignore them at your peril.

Chapter 9
The Little Things Can Be Huge

We played the same team for the state championship in back-to-back seasons. The first time we got some cheap foul calls on their star, confused their guards with our halfcourt trap and won pretty easily.

But the second time around, the opposition had recruited two new guards (it was a Catholic school, but still bringing in a USC-bound senior seemed a little over the line) and obviously was going to be prepared for our 1-3-1.

As we expected, the game was much closer, at least for the first half. Our presses and traps weren't as effective, but since we ran a pure motion offense with no set plays, they couldn't really prepare for that. The key to the game, though, was something so simple that we were stunned it worked so well. One of our several inbounds plays is called 'Box' and is designed to free up a player for a layup against a man-to-man. We ran it four times in the state title game and scored four baskets. We won by seven — so it doesn't take a calculator to figure out how important that play was.

We have a whole slew of inbounds plays, from underneath the basket, from the sidelines, from three-quarters court, and against a press. We try to score on every inbounds, and unless the defense is backed up protecting the basket, we don't settle for just getting the ball in. Against most good teams, we don't get much, granted, but one of the state championship banners hanging on that gym wall can be directly attributed to special plays, or, to use a football term, special teams.

As usual, I'm not promoting any particular set of plays, because there are a lot that work — including the famous 'barking dog' play, which is worth describing if only to prove that pushing the boundaries sometimes works wonders. This play actually occurred in a boys' state championship game, and it came with two seconds left in a one-point game. The trailing team had the ball out of bounds under its own basket. The offensive player directly in front of the inbounder waited until the ball was handed to the inbounder, and then fell to his knees and began barking like a dog. Another player on the inbounding team started at the weakside elbow and cut to the weakside block, where he was open for an easy layup because the opposition was staring at the barking 'dog' in utter befuddlement.

Hey, a win's a win.

But no matter what the inbounds play under the basket, make sure the girl inbounding the ball looks at her offensive teammate right in front of her. Two or three times a year, the defense will get completely confused, and our post player is standing on the block, unguarded, two feet away from the inbounder. Invariably, of course, our inbounder is looking somewhere else and we never convert. Make sure your players look to the block — you never know what you'll see there.

Another 'special team' is the press. Many teams press pretty much exclusively, but every team needs this arrow in the quiver, no matter how slow afoot it might be. The main reason is simply that sometimes the halfcourt game has resulted in a 15-point deficit midway through the second quarter, and changes must be made. The press can alter the tempo and the character of the game in no time.

Sure, maybe it will make that 15-point deficit 25, but if you're a team that only scores 50 a game, 15 points is Mt. Everest.

And you never know, you may just run into a team that's slower than you are, and the press might be just the ticket. A well-organized full or three-quarter court zone press can force turnovers, especially the first couple of times it's shown, and after that, it's easy to call it off. (Also, as mentioned previously about other aspects of the game, it's hard to practice against a press if you don't have one yourself. You need to install a press if only to assure that your kids can deal with it when they see it.)

Man presses, however, do require quickness, and so you need to keep your goals in mind before you commit to them. If you want to win a state title and your main weapon is a man press, then you better be quicker than all but one or two teams in the state — because sheer quickness can destroy a man press (witness the NBA). Of course, if your goal is just to have a good year in league (and depending on where you are in the process, that might be a great goal), and you're quicker than everyone else nearby, then go for it, and let the postseason take care of itself.

I've seen more than a few suburban pressing teams get to state and suddenly discover that the man press they love so much and that has worked so well, all of a sudden is vulnerable to the bigger postseason courts and quicker inner city players. A zone press, however, doesn't require as much of a physical advantage and can make up for some quickness deficits with anticipation and hustle. That said, though, every pressing team should have a man press, because man principles are the key to zone defense, and players must be ready to try and stop their opponents one-on-one.

Also, switching between man and zone presses is just as confusing to an offense as switching between man and zone in halfcourt — and if those quick guards have to think about what press they're facing, they won't be nearly as quick.

In terms of philosophy, the press is like any pressure defense: You give up coverage on the deep weakside in exchange for more people on the ball and in the easy passing lanes. And just as in zone defenses, you can pick the press that you understand the best or feel most comfortable with. It's less important which press you use than how you use it, and like anything else, you can't expect to press effectively unless you practice it.

The same, of course, is true of pressbreakers. We like to bring in older guys to press our girls' team in order to force them to face more pressure than they will in games, and the same tactic will work for boys' teams. (We run a three-on-four drill with three players trying to break a four-man press. At the start, they couldn't even get the ball across halfcourt — but after a few months, they became more confident and even scored now and again. It's a very tough drill for girls, but it's a very worthwhile one.)

There are a couple of generic ways to attack presses that will force some adjustments that will work to your advantage. The first is to bring all four non-inbounders up to the free-throw line, which pretty much requires one defender to stay deep to avoid long passes (and you should have some inbounds plays to burn the press if there isn't a deep defender). With that defender deep (and it's usually the person on the ball), now someone is unguarded. If it's the inbounder, she's got a great view of the various cutters, and if it's someone else, all she has to do is find the unguarded player and get her the ball. The next step is to just give the ball back to the inbounder or any guard who is left uncovered.

Since most teams send the person guarding the inbounder deep, put your best ballhandler as the inbounder and instruct whoever gets the ball to pass it directly back to her. Now you have your best ballhandler with the ball against the press, relatively unguarded.

Once you get into the pressbreaker, you should try to design it so the ballhandler always has three options: someone directly ahead of her, someone in the middle (since presses will force the ballhandler to one side or the other), and a safety behind her. (The safety's main responsibility is to create a good passing angle for the ballhandler. Sometimes the safety will stand there and expect the ballhandler to try and get her the ball by throwing over or through the defender, when all the safety has to do is take three steps to create a perfect angle for a bounce pass.) The best option is the middle, because that's where the press can be most effectively broken, but that leads to another philosophical issue.

Since we are a pressing, running team, we want the tempo as fast as possible. So we don't try to just break the press, we try to punish it. We want to get the ball to the middle, push the ball down the floor and score. If we turn it over due to that aggressiveness, well, that's OK because we're getting the game at our speed. But let's say you don't want to run with the team that's pressing you. Now you have a more subtle tempo problem. You still have to be aggressive to break the press, but your players have to understand that unless they're looking at a wide-open layup, they should pull back and get into their halfcourt offense. Pressing teams like to suck the opposition into a running game, and all of a sudden the slower team is gasping for breath and wondering how the lead got to 12.

Which leads to another point: Pressing teams, for the most part, are burst teams. That is, they will go along doing not too much, and then all of a sudden, they score a flurry of points in a very short span of time. These four- or eight- or 12-point bursts are what turn the game around, and the pressing coach shouldn't panic if things don't seem to be happening quickly enough. Sooner or later, a pressing team will get a burst of points, and if the game is even in the third quarter, the advantage lies with the pressers because they will have a burst or two left. On the other side of the scorer's table, pressbreaking coaches shouldn't hesitate at all to burn a timeout to stop a burst. If the press starts to smell blood, ten points can go up on the board in two minutes, especially if the pressers have any three-point shooters.

Speaking of three-point shooters, there's nothing like ending a quarter with a three-pointer as the buzzer sounds — and the best person to do that is a post player. If we have the ball with 30 seconds or less left in a quarter, we look for the last shot, and we want it to be a three. We have some set plays, but often we'll just run something called 'Four out,' which places four players beyond the arc and one player on the block. Players can penetrate and dish, or skip, and the one who usually has the best look is our post, because the other team's post naturally sags back into the middle. You can also run pick-and-rolls at the three-point line with the screener popping back out beyond the arc or any number of variations, but if that last-second three goes in, your team will get a huge boost, and the opposition will go way down. And if you miss the three, it's not devastating because it's a shot that doesn't usually go in.

If you've got plays for the end of the quarter, you should also have a couple of specials for the end of the game. You need a plan to get someone a shot if you have the ball at the opposite baseline with three seconds left, and one of your inbounds plays should generate a quick shot, both from the sidelines and underneath. The best way to work on these is to set up the game clock during practice now and again and spend some time with game-ending situations — including the last two minutes of a tie game (with or without teams in the bonus) as well as the last few seconds.

We also take five minutes a couple of times a year and have the kids practice half-court shots. You'd be amazed how much better they get after just practicing for a few minutes, and there's nothing like hitting one of those just before halftime to fire a team up. Besides, it's fun, and you can reward the player who makes the most long bombs by letting her skip the last liner or whatever motivation seems best for the team.

Another key special teams' play is the delay game, in those antediluvian states without the shot clock. You need to be prepared offensively and defensively to take advantage of late-game and late-quarter situations, and Mike Phelps of Bishop O'Dowd in California, a very successful coach, always used to hold the ball for the last minute of every quarter — because then when the fourth quarter came, his kids were confident they could run the delay game. It wasn't that much fun to watch in the first quarter (yet another reason to put in the shot clock), but it was very effective.

If you think about it, almost all of these special teams' efforts can be effective in putting points on the board and crucial in terms of wins and losses. There's never enough time to do everything you need to do, granted, but you can't just expect kids to produce on special teams unless they work on them — and remember those four baskets we got that won a state championship. It was a simple play, but we practiced it and refined it, and it won for us. Special teams can win for you too.

Chapter 10
Welcome to Postseason

So you've finally turned it around, and now your team is heading off to postseason play. It may not be your first trip, but none of the players have ever advanced this far before, and they don't know what to expect.

The first step, then, is psychological. It's crucial to lay out exactly what's going to happen, from unfamiliar refs to bigger crowds to more press coverage. Granted, that won't prepare them for the real thing, but at least it will let them know that it's a different level of play. (And regardless of how much experience you may have had in postseason, always stay cool and calm, no matter what happens. Make sure you read every handout word for word so that you know everything, from when you can get on the gym floor to how long halftime is. One year, we took a team to the regionals that had never played in an arena before, and we happened to be the first game. Tucked away in the official handout was, for some unknown reason, a paragraph that said the teams for the first game could be on the floor 90 minutes before the game, while for other games it was only 15 minutes. So we got those girls up there two hours before the game, had them change and were on the floor the second the 90-minute window opened. At first, the officials at the site refused to let us get on the court, but I had the handbook with me, pulled out the appropriate section, and all they could do was ask if we needed any basketballs. We then took an extended warmup, at both ends of the floor so that our kids were as familiar as possible with the unfamiliar surroundings.)

Once the game begins, officiating can be one of the most critical factors. In a state like California, refs may come from hundreds of miles away, and maybe have never seen the style of play you're used to — and your league refs are used to. They may call a lot more fouls, or hardly any at all. They may blow the whistle on every possible traveling violation, or never call it once.

The most important thing is that your kids can't let the refs take them out of the game. Warn them beforehand that they have to adjust to the officiating, not the other way around. If the first call is a ticky-tack hand-check, then everyone — coaches and players — has to go to school on it. If bodies fly on an offensive rebound and no whistle is heard, well, it's time to go to the boards with abandon. There's no use whining, and no time to waste. Whatever the refs do is what the refs do, as the old question explains: What's a foul? When the ref blows his whistle — no more and no less. Successful teams in postseason adjust to the officiating quickly and without wasting emotional energy on the way the game is called. Let the coaches work the refs; the players have to just play.

Crowd noise usually isn't a factor in the big games, which are often played in large college or professional arenas. There, the biggest difference is the length of the court and the background behind the basket. If at all possible, try to practice at a nearby college to get used to length of the court, and tell your shooters to focus on the front of the rim more than ever in those spacious arenas where there are no walls to establish depth perception. It does take some adjusting to get used to arenas, but until you've been there, don't make too big a deal of it — but if you've played in arenas more than your opponents, make sure your players know it. Confidence is always important in basketball, but especially so in postseason.

Before you get to arenas, though, and sometimes even in those caverns, there usually will be a game or two where crowd noise is a problem, and your team needs to be prepared. If you call most offensive and defensive sets, you might want to prepare some two-foot by three-foot posters with your play calls on them that an assistant coach can flash when needed. And it's especially important in postseason that when a play is signalled onto the court, in whatever manner, that the players make sure everyone knows what's been called. If one player doesn't know the play, that's the fault of the other four, not the one who didn't get the message.

Another way to get ready is to use the sound system in your gym, or some serious boom boxes, to crank up some annoying music. It shouldn't be music that the kids like, so put on some AC/DC or old disco at ear-splitting volume to give the players an idea of how it feels to play when they can't hear the coaches or each other.

Another issue is the media (or, as they are commonly known, the vultures of the press). When you're struggling, they're seldom around, settling for phone calls after games. (And make them, win or lose. Sportswriters have a tremendous amount to do with how a program is perceived, and not just by what they print. They talk to everyone, and their opinions are multiplied. If you only call in scores when you win, or call after deadline, you're making enemies you don't need to make.) Never, ever get in a spitting match with a local paper — as the old saying goes, don't get in an argument with anyone who buys ink by the barrel.

Once you start to win, though, reporters will start to show up more regularly, and some will want to do features on your star players.

At that moment, it's time to have a talk with the team, because jealousies that simmer just below the surface can erupt when a three-column color picture appears in the local paper. It's important for everyone involved with the program to understand that the press does what the press does, and there's nothing anyone can do about it.

If a sportswriter decides your point guard is the best point guard in the world, even though she's the third best in the league, and wants to do a feature on her, don't stand in his way. But make sure that everyone on the team knows that the point guard had nothing to do with the idea of the story. And make sure the point guard knows that she has to speak very carefully, especially about her own team. Sure, inadvertently putting down an opponent is bad news, but it's a lot worse if the point guard innocently says something that everyone knows to be true — 'Our posts have missed a lot of easy layups this year' — and it winds up in print. It sounds a lot different when it's in black and white.

Sportswriters are after stories, not the good of your program. It's not their job to make it easier for you to win or to curb the ego of your trigger-happy small forward. Newspapers have their own agendas, and high school coaches and players aren't going to change them. It is possible to subtly manipulate the press, but everybody tries to do that, all the time, and only the most inexperienced sportswriters will fall for anything insincere.

Radio and TV are less likely to have an impact on your team, but everyone on the team should understand that the way the media works is to emphasize individuals — and that's not the way teams work. An individual may get more press than she deserves, but that's not her doing and shouldn't affect the way the team interacts.

The press is in its own little world, and high school coverage is just a small part of it. The less seriously everybody takes it, the better.

The demands of the press will increase the further the team goes, as will community interest and outside pressures. By this time, though, all the hard work you've put in preparing your team will be paying off. The girls have traveled to hostile environments, so that's nothing new. They know how to get ready to play a game after a long bus ride or the day after a plane trip. They know how to get their rest in a motel or hotel, and when to get up, and when to eat.

And they know that what matters is what happens on the court, and that once you get on the court, it's just another game.

Well, sort of. Postseason basketball is different in several respects, and the most obvious one is that all the teams are good. The best team may not win, but a very good team will. And one thing good teams don't do is give up easy baskets. Pressing teams can crush weak opponents because of turnovers and an eventual mental collapse — but good teams will handle even the best press and won't buckle mentally.

Which means that postseason games are much more dependent on success in the halfcourt set than regular season games. To win a state title, you have to execute your offense and get good shots, which usually means your guards have to be mentally and physically up to the challenge. If your guards don't play well, your stay will be short.

But that doesn't mean the frontcourt is just along for the ride. Another mark of good teams is good defense, and good defense means lots of missed shots. Missed shots create rebounding opportunities, and there's nothing easier than a two-foot putback of a teammate's miss. To win in postseason, you absolutely must rebound, especially on the defensive end of the floor.

To summarize, the three keys to success are:

- Good guard play — your backcourt must handle pressure and keep the halfcourt offense rolling. A couple of threes or long jumpers wouldn't hurt either.
- Halfcourt execution — run the offense and make the 10-footers. If your team isn't totally organized offensively, points will be very hard to come by.
- Rebounding — if you don't get to the boards, start the bus and pick the date for your next open gym, because rebounding is what separates the champions from the rest.

There is one other very important aspect of postseason: Everybody has to have fun.

It's far too easy to treat the whole postseason journey as a life-or-death mission. Hey, the winners don't get any more money than the losers, and for most of these kids, just the chance to step on the same floor that was once trod by Vince Carter or Chamique Holdsclaw is a huge thrill — and they should be aware of it. Everyone should try to take some time to step back and enjoy being at this level, and take pride in the community support and the kids whose faces are painted in the school colors. Teams that are wound too tight almost always find a way to lose. The relaxed smiling team is the one that always scares me the most.

Speaking of smiling (but not necessarily relaxed), the better you get, the more you'll deal with college coaches. There's one simple rule here: Be honest. Don't tell a coach your point guard can get to the hoop as easily as she shoots threes if she doesn't even like to drive her car. Don't ignore your scorer's defensive weaknesses. In short, tell the truth, because in the long run, you do no one a service by telling a college coach a player can do things she can't.

And word gets around. If you oversell a player, then

other coaches are going to doubt you when you are sincerely convinced you have the next Sheryl Swoopes on your hands. And remember, all those coaches in the stands at the state tournament talk to each other, so if you mar your reputation with one coach, you've hurt yourself — and your players — with all of them.

It's been a long, long road to get to postseason, and whether you're eliminated in the first round or the last, make sure everyone understands what they've accomplished — even if many think the team should have gone farther. High school sports are about having fun, not about the one or two kids who will play in college (let's not even talk about the pros), and not about the press coverage, and the parents' obsession or the coaches' egos.

If you're not having fun in postseason and enjoying the ride, then it's definitely time to gear down. If the kids aren't having fun, you won't win anyway, so there's really no reason to take it all too seriously. The sun will still come up the next day, and most of your team will be back to do it all again next year.

Chapter 11
Parents: Blessing or Curse?

I remember standing in the locker room, commiserating with the athletic director over some particularly obnoxious father's attempt to get his daughter more playing time. 'Wouldn't it be great,' said the AD, staring off into space as if gazing upon the promised land, 'if they didn't have parents?'

There are times every coach knows that feeling all too well, but now that you have a successful program, parental and community involvement become more and more important, and more and more potentially destructive. To paraphrase an ancient saying, victory has a thousand parents, but defeat is an orphan. If you start to win, everybody will love you, or at least pretend to, and the pressure from parents will mount to keep on winning when their precious darlings are on the varsity.

One reason for this parental pressure is that your success is based on a tremendous commitment from the players, which means that parents are putting in time and spending money that they wouldn't on a less successful program. They're raising money (more on that later), hustling friends and businesses for new scoreboards and coming to all the games.

That last can be the most annoying, because after sitting in the stands for five or six games, all of a sudden you have a lot of experts who feel they can clearly see what the team needs and what the coaches are doing wrong. If you're not expected to win, then the carping from the crowd isn't that big a deal, but once you've established yourself, the intensity of the criticism rises.

And all parents want their kids to play. It is absolutely crucial to understand that every parent thinks their child is better than she is. A friend of mine, to give just one example, was sitting in the crowd at an elementary school concert, and pointed out her nine-year-old daughter. 'She's the cutest one on the stage, isn't she?' my friend asked. Sure, her daughter was cute, but there were some others that qualified as well — but her belief was unshakable that her daughter stood out above all the others. Now this was a woman who knows her daughter's limitations and is a teacher, yet motherly love clouded her vision.

Translated, this means that though it may be clear to you that little Anna can't dribble, shoot, pass or defend, Anna's dad thinks she just needs a little more time on the court or a little more encouragement to become a full-fledged star — or at least a starter. So it's critical to approach every conversation with a parent with complete confidence that even the smallest criticism will be misconstrued and that any innocent slip of the tongue will turn into an international incident.

Some coaches put it bluntly and tell parents that they won't talk about playing time and then don't mention it again. Others try to coat the pill of reality with plenty of sugar, but when it comes down to it, everyone can count minutes, and if little Anna gets two a game, it's pretty clear that you don't think she can play. However you decide to deal with parents who want to talk about playing time, be warned and be careful. Not talking about it at all can alienate key people who might otherwise be supporters; talking about it too much can force you to say things about their children that the parents don't want to hear.

So why keep parents happy at all? It's the kids who matter, right? Wrong. And not only wrong, but dangerously dead wrong. Any team that is truly successful has the committed support of some, if not all, of the parents. And if the parents party together, so much the better — if they're united, then a lot of problems that might otherwise land in your lap will get handled before they even come to your attention.

For example, if a dad is convinced his daughter should be getting more minutes and lets his hair down at a postgame party, he may discover that absolutely no one else agrees with him — and he then is much less likely to confront you. Or it's possible that one of the parents of the one of the starters will pull the dad aside later and try to calm him down, realizing that outspoken dissatisfaction of that sort can only lead to trouble later.

Most teams, officially or unofficially, have a team parent. That parent is as important as your lead assistant, and needs to feel as though he or she is part of the program. They should know what's happening ahead of time, if possible, and be in the loop on almost every aspect of the team. Most of the time, that parent needs to have a child who is a starter, because you don't want your team parent upset about playing time (the primary reason that parents hate coaches).

The process of dealing with parents begins with your selection of a team parent, who ideally is the parent of a freshman or sophomore who either starts or gets lots of playing time. The more time the team parent has with the program, the more efficiently everything will run. And it's hard to find a good team parent, so identifying one even when the player isn't on varsity yet is always a good idea.

The traditional preseason parent meeting is a critical event. You and your assistants should be there, and ideally there will be wine and food so that everyone is relaxed and reasonably happy. The parents need to bond just like the players do, and a party is often the best way. The parent meeting agenda should cover a lot of ground, from practice times to game schedules to travel necessities to meal times to fund-raising to statistics. The last two deserve a little more attention because of their importance in the big picture.

In some states, fund-raising is the sine qua non of a successful sports program. In those states, if you don't raise enough money, you can't travel or buy new uniforms or get enough new basketballs or get practice jerseys. Rich areas may have poor schools, so even if everyone's driving Porsches, you still may need to generate a lot of income. (One reason it's important to have money in the kitty, even in a rich community, is that there are always kids who are poorer, relatively speaking, than their teammates. Just because 10 of the parents can afford the Christmas trip doesn't mean all 12 can — and there needs to be a mechanism set up so that the kids and families who need extra financial help can get it. In some areas, new basketball shoes can be a substantial burden on a family's budget, and there need to be ways to address those kinds of problems, and those ways all require money in the bank.)

But even if your program is generously funded by the school district, it never hurts to go out and do some work on your own. The kids should be involved at some level so they understand what it takes to run the program. Ideally you want to generate the most income with the smallest investment of time and energy. If you can get a local merchant to buy all the kids bags, that's an easy way to accomplish a specific goal. If you need $1,500 for new uniforms, you can try to put together car washes and bake sales (always sell the tickets in advance rather than settle for promises to show up). But if you need to raise several thousand dollars, you run the risk of burning out your parents and kids with an endless series of fund-raisers. So if you need big dollars, you have to go for high-return events.

One way is to look for corporate and community funding. In poorer areas, where the community may not have enough money to really help, try convincing big corporations to step in as a sign of their involvement with all levels of society. The local hairdresser can't help you that much, but if you can get McDonald's or Chevron or the Bank of America involved, then you might be able to get one big check and get it all done. It's important to remember, though, that it takes a lot of time to get things done at the corporate level — and they will be looking for a track record as well. After you've put together a decent program, you can approach a big company, but realize it will be at least a year before you see any return. Still, if it does come through, you've solved a lot of problems with one concentrated effort instead of 15 car washes.

In richer areas, the parents might work for, or have connections with, large corporations, which may help, but generally big companies will pass on giving money to relatively affluent high schools. In those cases, you need to come up with a money-making plan that doesn't require massive hours of volunteer involvement — and that's no easy task. Some schools have a huge barbeque or crab feed with donated (or discount) food and lots of volunteer labor. The key here is publicity and getting the community excited, and it doesn't hurt to have a big-name speaker (the local college basketball coach, who will be even happier to come if you show him the D-1 prospects who are just entering school).

Another avenue is a shootout, as opposed to a tournament. A shootout is a one-day event with six or seven games, hopefully involving at least one big-time game between regionally and/or nationally ranked teams. The bulk of the games should involve local teams, because that's who will come to the games, but what you really want is for those fans to stick around to see the marquee game — and buy lots of sodas and hot dogs while they're waiting. With good teams, good press and good luck, a one-day event can generate a couple thousand dollars, and it's not a killer in terms of energy expenditure. Everybody has to give up the one day for the shootout, but if it's successful enough, that may be all you need to do.

Tournaments can also generate money, but they take up much more time and produce less per hour than shootouts. You can make a small profit from the entry fee (in the shootout, everyone plays for free), but a typical eight-team event is three very long days with lots of games where there are not a lot of fans, and very little concessions revenue. Still, properly done, they can be a definite profit center, but go in realizing that you need a cadre of dedicated volunteers who will spend eight hours for three straight days without complaint.

In the end, though, your best fund-raising option will be determined by your own community and your parents. If one of your parents owns a restaurant, all sorts of ideas are now possible that weren't before; and similarly if one of them has a brother who's a vice-president with Burger King. What you need to do is to calculate the number of volunteer hours per dollar in return and try to find the one that takes up the least amount of time.

Obviously, the more successful your program, the easier it is to make money. And it doesn't hurt if your team plays a run-and-gun style that's fun to watch. If people come to the games and have a good time, they might come back — and they'll start to identify with the team. That means when the fund-raisers come around, they'll be more likely to get involved, and contribute time or money.

And what will you spend the money on? Warmups, equipment bags, shoes, a new scoreboard (which will make you friends with every other coach who uses the gym), new uniforms, travel, practice equipment, glass backboards for the side courts, a contribution toward getting three-point lines painted for each basket, etc. There's no shortage of things to buy if you have the money — including a computerized statistical system.

Those handy little devices are more and more common in recent years, and though they take a dedicated operator who will see little of the game, and one or two faithful helpers, they will produce stats that will help you as a coach, and help your players get to college. Accurate statistics are a necessity, however you get them, and your parents are going to have to keep them, computer or no computer. Maybe you can convince the math class to get involved, or you've got a cousin who just loves numbers. Most likely, though, it's the parents, and there some things to remember. Don't have the point guard's father keep the assist chart, or the center's mother tally rebounds. And make sure that whoever does minutes played is the parent of a starter — you don't want dad realizing little Anna got 30 seconds for the third straight game. (Why keep minutes played? Because the most valuable statistics are points per minute or 32 minutes, depending on your preference, rebounds per minute, etc. Sure, the starters are going to rack up the raw numbers, but if you keep per-minute stats, you might be surprised to learn that your backup forward gets more rebounds per minute than the starter and might deserve to play more.)

Regardless of how you do it, though, parents must commit to keeping stats as accurately as humanly possible. The team parent or a designated stat parent should hand out the clipboards with the stat forms (along with sharpened pencils with erasers) before every game and hand them to one of the coaches afterward. The stats will help you give the press more details when you call in the score ('Jane Jumpshot had 12 rebounds and three steals to go along with her 14 points') and will also obviously give you a better idea of who played well. For college coaches, legitimate statistics are tremendously valuable, and they will help your players go where they want to go.

But the most important thing your parents do is not raise money or keep stats. They are the program's voice in the community, and they are the program's support system. If they are sold on the team and your coaching, then they'll tell everyone so and they'll generate community enthusiasm. If they believe in what you're doing, they'll get the kids to the games, they won't complain about the time demands, and they'll be there for you when things go wrong. Ideally, they will all like each other and go down to the pizza parlor after big games and dissect what went on over pepperoni and a couple of pitchers.

The struggling team doesn't have too many parent problems because the parents probably don't care that much. But the successful team will attract parents because of that success, and they will expect more for their children. If you can deliver and keep everybody reasonably happy, the parents will be almost as important to your program as the players. But if they're unhappy, inevitably the players will be too — and eventually that will show up in the standings.

Chapter 12
Getting There is Easier Than Staying There

So you've made it. The banner hangs on the wall in the gym, the postseason banquet was a rousing success with parents, players and coaches all basking in the afterglow of achievement.

Now what?

First, the old saying is true: It is much harder to stay there than it is to get there. Once you're a champion, once you're a name, every night out you're the hunted, not the hunter. Once you've won that title, anything less is a disappointment. At the beginning, two wins in the postseason were a cause for celebration; now, two wins in postseason is a bitter pill for everyone to swallow. And victory no longer tastes as sweet, because it's expected. Conversely, defeat is more sour than ever, for with it comes the questions, the un-lived-up-to expectations and the passive minutes watching the other team dance on the court.

There are many coaches who call it quits at the first blush of success, and it's hard to blame them. They've accomplished something special, they've worked very hard, they've made many sacrifices, and they're tired. And, very often, the talent is graduating too, so with a couple years of struggle ahead, it hardly seems worth it to keep going.

If you feel that way, you too should hang it up. There's no guilt, as long as you haven't made promises, but know that your program will most likely fade with your departure. An enduring high school program requires a decade of success, at the least, and if you want your legacy to be more than just a banner, you'll have to stick around.

By now, you should have a steady stream of skilled, if not necessarily talented, players coming into the school, and most of them should be familiar with your style of play and what you will demand from them and their families. In addition, they should know a lot of your system by participating in summer leagues and through your feeder programs. This kind of talent may not generate a league title, but it will guarantee a winning season, at the worst. The players are ready and willing to do what's necessary to keep the tradition going, and they will take pride in making their own contribution.

But the engine that drives the program is you, and the fires must still burn in you. You still have to be excited about the first day of practice and enjoy seeing the younger players move up. The summer season must be more than a chore, and though some aspects of the job may become more onerous as time goes on, you still have to be enthusiastic in your heart, you still have to want to build a program that will be remembered in the community for decades to come. And you still have to love the game and love working with teenagers, teaching them, and helping them move on.

You cannot expect your relationship with your former players to be much more than perfunctory. They will come back to some games, perhaps, and chat in the grocery store, but don't expect any flowery speeches when one of your players does something exceptional in college, or long letters acknowledging your profound influence on their lives.

When they graduate, they're gone, and the new players are the ones who you must focus on — and they, in turn, will move on as well.

The rewards of continued success are many, ranging from your own internal sense of satisfaction at a job well done to recognition in the basketball community at large. Your players will benefit, for they will find it easier to get into colleges, whether they earn a scholarship or not, and they will learn that hard work is the surest road to success, a lesson as valuable as any a school can teach.

But to keep that going, you must keep working hard yourself. The day you coast is the day your program starts to slip, because if you're coasting, your players will inevitably start coasting too. There's no substitute for commitment and hard work, at any level of basketball or at any level of life. What you work at is what you're good at, and if you work hard on your basketball program, it will be a good one.

Success, though, is not without its pitfalls. When you're a struggling program, no one pays any attention to what you do. You can practice out of season, informally recruit players and scream on the sidelines and no one will really care. But once you start winning — especially if you displace a traditional power — expect increased scrutiny. The wolves will be out, looking for any weakness they can attack and any regulation you might have broken.

It's always critical to follow the rules, and not just for moral reasons, though that should be justification enough. What are you teaching your players if your program cheats in order to win? How much do you really gain from that extra practice? Is that gain really worth the cost, even if you never get caught? But if you succeed, and you cheat, you will get caught, plain and simple. All eyes will be on you, and when a player doesn't make the varsity when she thinks she should, Dad may call the school board and complain about those 'open gyms' that are actually shooting drills. And parents from opposing schools who might be on your campus for a meeting will be sure to report anything suspicious. (We got in trouble one year because we were coaching a postseason all-star team, which included a couple of our players. An assistant coach from another program, who knew nothing of the all-star game, saw the practice and called our principal, which eventually led to a school board meeting claiming we were practicing out of season.)

In the long run, doing everything by the book pays off over and over again. Then there's no need to worry about what people say, inside or outside the program, because there's nothing to hide. And there's no taint on any accomplishment, either by the players or the coaches, because all the rules have been followed from day one.

And there will be accomplishments. A coach who builds a program from nothing and stays on for a decade or more, will become a respected member of the community, as well as an influential figure in the local basketball world. Postseason honors will multiply, invitations to clinics and to coach all-star teams will show up in the mailbox, and the widening pool of graduated players will serve as living proof of the program's impact on young people's lives.

Will you get rich too? Sadly, no, but if you started coaching high school basketball in order to get rich, you definitely went left when you should have gone right. There's big money to be made in the upper echelons of the professional and collegiate game, and it's possible that the architect of a powerful high school program can rise that high. It's not likely, however, just as it's not likely that any of your players will ever play in the NBA or WNBA. Such long-range goals can't be the source of your drive.

In the end, as the old commercials said, you've got to have the love. You've got to love the practices, the scheduling, the games, the people and everything that goes into building a winning program. You've got to love the process of success, not just the success itself, because if you don't, it won't happen. It's a hard road, with some nasty potholes and some gorgeous vistas, but you can't have one without the other.

After all, the success of your program isn't in your won-loss records or that state championship, or that all-star coaching gig or even in the scholarships you helped your players earn. If you stay true to yourself, listen to your heart, and try to stay in touch with the love you have for the game and the people who share it with you, success is all but guaranteed — and the satisfaction and joy will be as sweet and pure as a three-pointer that hits nothing but net.